Flowersmith

For Ferdinand

Flowersmith

HOW TO HANDCRAFT AND ARRANGE ENCHANTING PAPER FLOWERS

JENNIFER TRAN

FOREWORD BY RICHARD ALOISIO

hardie grant books

Contents

Foreword

Pliers, scissors, scallop edgers, bamboo skewers, toothpicks — what on earth do these items have to do with the uncommon beauty of the photographs held within the pages of this book?

Let's back up a bit first. Permit me to give a brief history of my admiration for the enormously talented Jennifer Tran. I chanced upon Jennifer's paper flowers on Instagram one day in February of 2015. I love colour and design, and was immediately drawn to her posts. I was new to Instagram and simply 'liked' her posts for a number of weeks, until I got up the courage to write my first comment: 'Incredible work and brilliant gallery'. With that statement, I began following Jennifer's feed and writing words of praise on her posts often. Sometimes I'd give her post a whimsical title, sometimes I'd comment on her superb lighting skills, sometimes I'd tell her what a gifted artist she was. Jennifer always replied to my words with a grace and appreciation that, quite frankly, I found delightful.

In a very short time, Jennifer was following my feed and we established a friendship and a mutual admiration for each other's talents — which has culminated with her request that I write the foreword to the book you now hold in your hands!

I've had the great pleasure and humbling experience of being the recipient of a number of amazing gifts from Jennifer: three delicate lapel flowers for my (many) suits were the first pieces I marvelled at; and just recently I received a magnificent giant red peony that now stands regally in a vase on my dining-room table.

One of the things that strikes me about Jennifer's extraordinary work is that her desire for perfection is unlimited. Just scroll through her Instagram gallery or flick through the pages of this book and you'll see what I mean.

I have a confession. I actually cannot look at Jennifer's work for too long; it's just too gorgeous. My senses get overloaded with colour and beauty and I get a little weak at the knees and a whole lot envious. It continues to amaze me that with just some paper and the mundane tools mentioned above she is able to create such intensely beautiful works of art.

With this book, Jennifer shares her creativity, knowledge and techniques, so that you too will be able to create some of her wonderful projects.

I think there is an air of magic around art like this, which I can't help but admire and cherish. Inside this book is all you need to make your own magic — and it will most certainly be admired and cherished by all who see it!

Very sincerely

RICHARD ALOISIO
ART DIRECTOR, *THE NEW YORK TIMES*

Introduction

Welcome to the wonderful world of paper flowers, where you hold the magic to create beauty, to inspire and to bring excitement to the lives of everyone around you. Imagine the smile on someone's face when you give them a beautiful bloom that you have crafted with love. Imagine how that smile could warm your heart and make you feel like you've done something so right. The warm fuzzy feeling may not last forever but the flower will, and it will always be a reminder of that happy moment.

In this book, I will give you a helping hand to create that magic. It doesn't matter whether you are new to crafting or have been doing it for years, *Flowersmith* will be your kind crafting companion. I will share with you everything I know about flower making, from the basic skills, to how to understand flower structure, and where to get the best supplies for amazing results. You will learn how to construct paper flowers, ranging from the most effortless bloom to highly complex arrangements where your judgement and individuality will come into play.

I have structured the book in a way that allows you to start any project without having to read the book from the beginning. At the start of each flower and foliage project, I list the required skills, which are explained in detail in the Skills chapter (page 242). I encourage you to read the relevant sections as you start working on your first project, because it will give you context to better understand and retain the information.

Each project includes numbered step-by-step instructions, with corresponding photographs for many of the steps (look for the shaded circle behind the step number, then match it to the step number in the corner of the photo). The templates are all on single-sided pages, so you can cut them directly from the book if you wish.

Note that the difficulty level given at the beginning of each project is an indication only, and is designed to grade the range of projects included in this book. It is not an indication of your skill level — which I guarantee will improve immensely after you work through *Flowersmith*. I hope that by the time you finish with this book, you will be able to look at any flower and immediately discover its structure and know exactly how to create your own templates.

As I often say to my Instagram followers, I have one guiding principle in flower making: *flaunt your flaws*. You will find that even if you use the same templates as the person sitting next to you, your flowers will always be unique. As with natural flowers, no two paper flowers can ever be the same — and doesn't it make life more exciting! Some flowers that you make will appear perfect to your eye, while others may seem to be missing some elements, but what they will all have in common is that they are uniquely yours. Embrace them!

Arra

ngements

Sunshine

Lily & Fringed Tulip

FLOWERS & FOLIAGE

3 Lilies with buds: flowers varied lengths 25–30 cm (10–12 in), buds varied lengths 40–45 cm (16–18 in) (Flower 15, page 151)

1–2 Lilies without buds, varied lengths 25–30 cm (10–12 in) (Flower 15, page 151)

8 Fringed Tulips in salmon, varied lengths 25–35 cm (10–14 in) (Flower 10, page 121)

MATERIALS

– Parafilm tape

NOTE

Lilies and Tulips are both complex projects, so allow yourself plenty of time.

1. Bunch all the Lilies together so that the flowers and buds lean slightly towards the left. Secure the stems using parafilm tape.

2. Bend the Tulip stems so that they lean in the same direction as the Lilies.

3. Add the Tulips to the left side of the arrangement and secure using parafilm tape.

4. If you wish, bend the stems further for a more natural look.

Clematis & Gardenia

FLOWERS & FOLIAGE

7–9 Clematis vines in fuchsia,
varied lengths 35–40 cm (14–16 in)
(Flower 4, page 85)

1 Clematis vine in fuchsia,
50 cm (20 in) tall (Flower 4, page 85)

7 Gardenias without foliage,
varied lengths 25–35 cm (10–14 in)
(Flower 11, page 127)

1. Arrange the short and medium Clematis vines in a vase so that they lean in different directions.

2. Place the tall Clematis vine in the centre of the arrangement.

3. Position the Gardenias among the short and medium Clematis vines.

4. Bend the stems gently to create a natural look.

Delphinium & Cosmos

FLOWERS & FOLIAGE

3 Delphinium sprigs in electric blue,
varied lengths 45–50 cm (18–20 in)
(Flower 8, page 109)

3 Delphinium sprigs in midnight blue,
varied lengths 40–45 cm (16–18 in)
(Flower 8, page 109)

30–35 Cosmoses, varied lengths 25–40 cm
(10–16 in) (Flower 5, page 91)

1. Arrange the electric-blue Delphiniums in a vase so that they lean in different directions.

2. Position the midnight-blue Delphiniums in front of the electric-blue ones.

3. Place 25 to 30 of the Cosmoses in the front and centre of the arrangement.

4. Add the remaining Cosmoses between the two layers of Delphiniums, making sure the Cosmoses are at different heights.

Cosmos, Juliet Rose & Open Rose

FLOWERS & FOLIAGE

20–25 Cosmoses, varied lengths 25–30 cm
(10–12 in) (Flower 5, page 91)

5–6 Juliet Roses in yellow without
foliage, varied lengths 20–30 cm
(8–12 in) (Flower 13, page 139)

15–17 Open Roses in yellow without
foliage, varied lengths 25–30 cm
(10–12 in) (Flower 18, page 169)

9–10 Basic Branches, varied lengths
20–25 cm (8–10 in) (Foliage 2, page 212)

MATERIALS

– Parafilm tape
– Ribbon (optional)

NOTE

For a small and effortless posy, reduce
the number of flowers.

1. Bunch together five mixed flowers in no particular arrangement and secure the stems with parafilm tape.

2. Gradually build the bouquet by adding more flowers around the first bunch, securing the stems with parafilm tape as you go.

3. Position the Basic Branches around the base of the bouquet and secure with parafilm tape.

4. Cover the parafilm tape with ribbon if you wish.

Nasturtium Wreath

FLOWERS & FOLIAGE

2 Nasturtium vines in orange/tangerine
(Flower 17, page 163)

MATERIALS

– 18-gauge wire
– Parafilm tape
– 60gsm crepe paper strip in light green
– PVA glue

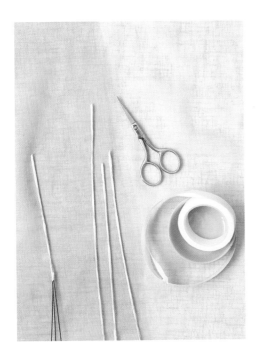

1. Bunch three 45 cm (18 in) pieces of wire together and wrap them with parafilm tape. Repeat to make three more stems. Using parafilm tape, join the top half of one stem to the bottom half of another.

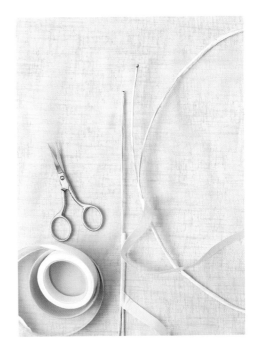

2. Join on the remaining stems in the same way. Bend the resulting length of wire to create a circle, joining the top half of the first stem to the bottom half of the last stem using parafilm tape.

3. Wrap the entire circle with light-green paper strip and secure with PVA glue.

4. Using parafilm tape, attach the Nasturtiums to the circular frame. Cover the joins with light-green paper strip. Bend the flowers and leaves to create a natural look.

Harvest

Dahlia & Zinnia

FLOWERS & FOLIAGE

5 Dahlias in crimson, varied lengths
20–30 cm (8–12 in) (Flower 7, page 103)

7 Zinnias in red/wine, varied lengths
20–30 cm (8–12 in) (Flower 23, page 199)

2 Basic Vines, varied lengths 25–30 cm
(10–12 in) (Foliage 4, page 222)

4 Basic Vines, varied lengths 40–50 cm
(16–20 in) (Foliage 4, page 222)

2 Basic Vines, varied lengths 55–60 cm
(22–24 in) (Foliage 4, page 222)

3 Dahlias in yellow-salmon gradient,
varied lengths 25–35 cm (10–14 in)
(Flower 7, page 103)

3 Dahlias in salmon, varied lengths
25–35 cm (10–14 in) (Flower 7, page 103)

3 Zinnias in lilac/orchid, varied lengths
20–35 cm (8–14 in) (Flower 23, page 199)

2 Zinnias in lilac/orchid, varied lengths
40–45 cm (16–18 in) (Flower 23, page 199)

NOTE

To create the yellow-salmon gradient
paper, use the dry-wash technique (see
Colouring 1, page 247) with yellow food
dye and salmon paper.

This is a big project, so allow yourself
plenty of time.

1. Arrange the crimson Dahlias in a vase, so that they lean towards the left. Add the red/wine Zinnias, arranging them so that they lean towards the right. Position all of the Basic Vines behind the flowers.

2. Position the yellow-salmon Dahlias so their heads are above the crimson Dahlias.

3. Place the salmon Dahlias in the centre of the arrangement.

4. Position the short lilac/orchid Zinnias among the crimson and salmon Dahlias. Finish by placing the tall lilac/orchid Zinnias among the taller Basic Vines.

Magnolia Grandiflora

FLOWERS & FOLIAGE

5–6 Magnolia Grandiflora, 30–40 cm
(12–16 in) (Flower 16, page 157)

MATERIALS

– Parafilm tape

– Ribbon (optional)

1. Select the Magnolia Grandiflora with the longest stem to be in the centre of the arrangement.

2. Arrange the remaining flowers evenly around the first flower.

3. Secure the stems using parafilm tape.

4. Cover the tape with ribbon if you wish.

Maple Leaf & Hypericum Berry Swag

FLOWERS & FOLIAGE

3–5 Maple Leaf sprigs in wine,
varied lengths 40–45 cm (16–18 in)
(Foliage 7, page 233)

2–3 Maple Leaf sprigs in red,
varied lengths 35–40 cm (14–16 in)
(Foliage 7, page 233)

3–5 Hypericum Berry sprigs, varied lengths
25–30 cm (10–12 in) (Foliage 6, page 229)

MATERIALS

– Parafilm tape

– Paper twine or a wide ribbon

1. Bunch the wine-coloured Maple Leaf sprigs together, making sure that the longest branch is in the centre. Use parafilm tape to secure the stems.

2. Arrange the red Maple Leaf sprigs over the wine-coloured ones and secure the stems with parafilm tape.

3. Layer the Hypericum Berry sprigs over the Maple Leaves and secure the stems with parafilm tape.

4. Cover the parafilm tape with paper twine or a wide ribbon.

Dahlia & Japanese Anemone

FLOWERS & FOLIAGE

5 Dahlias in crimson, varied lengths
20–25 cm (8–10 in) (Flower 7, page 103)

6–7 Japanese Anemones in white/bubblegum,
varied lengths 25–45 cm (10–18 in)
(Flower 12, page 133)

2–3 incomplete Japanese Anemones in
white/bubblegum with 2–3 petals each,
varied lengths 20–40 cm (8–16 in)
(Flower 12, page 133)

Basic Branches (Foliage 2, page 212)
(optional)

NOTE

For a fuller table centrepiece, add more
flowers. You could also use Basic Branches
as filler to hold the flowers in place.

1. Put the Dahlias in a vase.

2. Start adding the complete Japanese Anemones, paying attention to the direction of the buds.

3. Continue adding the complete Japanese Anemones, arranging them so that all the buds lean in the same direction.

4. For the finishing touch, add the incomplete Japanese Anemones to the arrangement.

Chrysanthemum & Clematis

FLOWERS & FOLIAGE

7–9 Chrysanthemums in violet,
varied lengths 25–35 cm (10–14 in)
(Flower 3, page 79)

3 Chrysanthemums in lilac,
varied lengths 20–35 cm (8–14 in)
(Flower 3, page 79)

5–7 Clematis vines in fuchsia,
varied lengths 30–45 cm (12–18 in)
(Flower 4, page 85)

1. Arrange the violet Chrysanthemums in a vase so that they lean in different directions.

2. Arrange the lilac Chrysanthemums among the violet Chrysanthemums.

3. Position the Clematis vines among the Chrysanthemums.

4. Gently bend the Clematis vines to create a natural look.

Frost

Olive Branch & Daffodil

FLOWERS & FOLIAGE

7 Olive Branches, varied lengths
20–45 cm (8–18 in) (Foliage 8, page 239)

8–12 Daffodils in vanilla,
varied lengths 20–35 cm (8–14 in)
(Flower 6, page 97)

NOTE

For a more colourful arrangement, use
yellow paper for the Daffodil coronas and
apply the wet-wash technique using orange
food dye (see Colouring 1, page 247).

1. Put the short Olive Branches in a vase.

2. Gradually build your arrangement by adding the tall Olive Branches.

3. Arrange the Olive Branches so they lean in different directions.

4. Position the Daffodils among the Olive Branches.

Camellia

FLOWERS & FOLIAGE

2–3 Basic Branches, varied lengths
25–30 cm (10–12 in) (Foliage 2, page 212)

2–3 Basic Branches, varied lengths
40–50 cm (16–20 in) (Foliage 2, page 212)

1–2 Basic Branches, varied lengths
55–60 cm (22–24 in) (Foliage 2, page 212)

5 Camellias in peach-blossom pink without
leaves and buds, varied lengths 20–30 cm
(8–12 in) (Flower 2, page 73)

3 Camellias in coral with leaves and buds,
varied lengths 25–35 cm (10–14 in)
(Flower 2, page 73)

10 Camellias in sweet-pea (buds optional),
varied lengths 20–45 cm (8–18 in)
(Flower 2, page 73)

NOTE

As this is quite a large arrangement,
use a stable vase with a heavy base.

1. Arrange all the branches in a vase so that they lean in different directions.

2. Add the peach-blossom pink Camellias, so that most of them lean slightly towards the right.

3. Position the coral Camellias on the left of the arrangement.

4. Position the sweet-pea Camellias among the other flowers and branches.

Eucalyptus Branch, Air Plant, Anemone & Hypericum Berry

FLOWERS & FOLIAGE

1 Eucalyptus Branch, 60 cm (24 in) tall
(Foliage 5, page 225)

3 Eucalyptus Branches, 50 cm (20 in) tall
(Foliage 5, page 225)

4–5 Eucalyptus Branches, varied lengths
30–40 cm (12–16 in) (Foliage 5, page 225)

1 Air Plant, 25 cm (10 in) tall
(Foliage 1, page 207)

5 Anemones in white, varied lengths
20–30 cm (8–12 in) (Flower 1, page 67)

3–5 Hypericum Berry sprigs,
varied lengths 10–30 cm (4–12 in)
(Foliage 6, page 229)

1. Arrange all the Eucalyptus Branches in a vase so that they lean in different directions.

2. Place the Air Plant in the centre of the arrangement.

3. Position the Anemones around the Air Plant.

4. Arrange the Hypericum Berry sprigs among the Anemones and around the Air Plant.

Leucadendron & Eucalyptus

FLOWERS & FOLIAGE

7 Leucadendrons in red/green, varied
lengths 25–35 cm (10–14 in)
(Flower 14, page 145)

3–5 Leucadendrons in yellow/green,
varied lengths 25–35 cm (10–14 in)
(Flower 14, page 145)

4–5 Eucalyptus Branches, varied lengths
20–35 cm (8–14 in) (Foliage 5, page 225)

MATERIALS

– Parafilm tape

– Ribbon (optional)

1. Bunch half of the red/green Leucadendrons together and secure using parafilm tape.

2. Add the yellow Leucadendrons to the bunch and secure with parafilm tape.

3. Add the remaining red Leucadendrons and secure with parafilm tape.

4. Position the Eucalyptus Branches around the outside of the arrangement and secure with parafilm tape. Cover the tape with a ribbon if you wish.

Peony, Plum Blossom & Cosmos

FLOWERS & FOLIAGE

3–4 Peonies in sweet-pea, 30 cm (12 in) tall (Flower 19, page 175)

3 Peonies in white, 30 cm (12 in) tall (Flower 19, page 175)

6–8 Plum Blossom branches, varied lengths 40–50 cm (16–20 in) (Flower 20, page 181)

NOTE

Use the edge-drawing technique on several of the white Peony petals (see Colouring 2, page 247).

1. Arrange all the Peonies in a vase so that they lean in different directions.

2. Position the Plum Blossoms in the centre of the arrangement.

3. Bend the stems of the Plum Blossoms so that they lean in different directions.

4. If you wish, turn this arrangement into a grand centrepiece by adding more flowers.

Bloom

Gardenia & Sweet Pea

FLOWERS & FOLIAGE

1 Gardenia with leaves and bud,
25 cm (10 in) tall (Flower 11, page 127)

1 Gardenia with flower only,
20 cm (8 in) tall (Flower 11, page 127)

1 Gardenia with flower only,
25 cm (10 in) tall (Flower 11, page 127)

20 Sweet Pea stems, varied lengths
30–45 cm (12–18 in) (Flower 22, page 193)

NOTE

As there are a lot of petals required to make the Sweet Peas for this project, I recommend that you cut, cup and curl the petals in batches. To avoid mix-ups, make sure to keep a separate pile of petals for each template.

1. Put the three Gardenias in a vase, positioning the flower with leaves and bud front and centre.

2. Add the Sweet Peas, arranging them so that their heads are higher than the Gardenias.

3. Gently bend the stems of several Sweet Peas to create a natural look.

4. If you wish, turn this arrangement into a grand centrepiece by adding more flowers.

Peony & Eucalyptus Branch

FLOWERS & FOLIAGE

3 Peonies in pink, varied lengths
35–40 cm (14–16 in) (Flower 19, page 175)

3 Peonies in white, varied lengths
20–25 cm (8–10 in) (Flower 19, page 175)

1 Eucalyptus Branch, 60 cm (24 in) tall
(Foliage 5, page 225)

3 Eucalyptus Branches, 50 cm (20 in) tall
(Foliage 5, page 225)

4–5 Eucalyptus Branches,
varied lengths 30–40 cm (12–16 in)
(Foliage 5, page 225)

NOTE

Use the edge-drawing technique on several
of the white Peony petals (see Colouring
2, page 247).

To make a bouquet, reduce the number of
flowers and add the short Eucalyptus
Branches to the base of the arrangement.

1. Arrange all the Peonies in a vase so that they lean in different directions.

2. Gently bend the tops of the Eucalyptus Branches to create a natural look.

3. Add the Eucalyptus Branches to the arrangement one by one, positioning them evenly around the Peonies.

4. If you wish, turn this arrangement into a grand centrepiece by adding more flowers and foliage.

Dogwood & Anemone

FLOWERS & FOLIAGE

4–5 Dogwood branches in pink, varied lengths 30–45 cm (12–18 in) (Flower 9, page 115)

1 Dogwood branch in pink, 60 cm (24 in) tall (Flower 9, page 115)

12 Anemones in peach-blossom pink, varied lengths 25–40 cm (10–16 in) (Flower 1, page 67)

MATERIALS

- Parafilm tape

NOTE

I recommend that the Anemones be a stronger and brighter shade of pink than the Dogwoods, as the Anemones are the focal flowers in this arrangement.

To create light-pink Dogwoods, use the dry-wash technique (see Colouring, page 247) with rose-pink food dye and white paper.

1. Join two of the shorter Dogwood branches
to the tallest Dogwood branch, securing
with parafilm tape.

2. Arrange all the Dogwood branches in a
vase, with the tallest branch in the
centre.

3. Position the Anemones among the Dogwood
branches.

4. For an even more stable arrangement, fill
the middle and lower sections with more
Anemones.

BLOOM 4

Peony & Poppy

FLOWERS & FOLIAGE

4–5 Peonies in pink,
varied lengths 30–35 cm (12–14 in)
(Flower 19, page 175)

7 Poppies in yellow, varied lengths
40–45 cm (16–18 in) (Flower 21, page 187)

3 Poppies in orange, varied lengths
37–42 cm (14½–16½ in)
(Flower 21, page 187)

3 Poppy buds in orange, varied lengths
40–45 cm (16–18 in)
(Flower 21, page 187)

1. Arrange the Peonies in a vase so that they lean in different directions.

2. Place the yellow Poppies in the centre of the arrangement.

3. Position the orange Poppies and Poppy buds among the yellow Poppies.

4. If you wish, bend the stems further for a more natural look.

Fringed Tulip & Basic Branch

FLOWERS & FOLIAGE

14–15 Fringed Tulips in yellow,
varied lengths 25–40 cm (10–16 in)
(Flower 10, page 121)

3 Basic Branches, varied lengths
55–60 cm (22–24 in) (Foliage 2, page 212)

4 Basic Branches, varied lengths
40–50 cm (16–20 in) (Foliage 2, page 212)

2–3 Basic Branches, varied lengths
25–30 cm (10–12 in) (Foliage 2, page 212)

MATERIALS

- Cotton twine

NOTE

This project calls for Tulips in yellow,
but feel free to go wild with your colour
choice.

1. Gently bend the Basic Branches to create a natural look.

2. Bunch together the longest Basic Branches with half of the Fringed Tulips.

3. Secure the stems using cotton twine.

4. Position the remaining Fringed Tulips and medium Basic Branches evenly around the outside of the arrangement. Add the short Basic Branches randomly around the outside and secure with twine.

Anatomy

1. **CALYX & SEPALS**
   A calyx is a set of pointy sepals (typically 3-5), often curled outwards, attached to the base of the flower. In some flower projects, such as Plum Blossom and Delphinium, individual sepals are used to cover buds.

2. **TENDRIL**
   Tendrils are thin spirals made from 22-gauge wire. They can be attached to climbing plants such as Sweet Pea and Clematis.

3. **PETAL**
   Petals are often the focal point of a flower. When making a large bouquet, create a natural look by adding some incomplete flowers with less than the specified number of petals.

4. **CENTRE**
   Centres are often made of cotton wool covered with crepe paper. Not all flowers in this book have a centre.

5. **STAMEN**
   There are two types of stamens used in this book: artificial (bought) and handmade. Handmade stamens are often made by wrapping fringed paper evenly around the centre.

6. **BUD**
   Buds can be round or cone-shaped, and are covered by a layer of sepals. Not all arrangements call for buds, but you can add them if you wish.

7. **NODE**
   A node (or joint) is the point where a leaf stem or flower stem joins the main stem or branch.

8. **BRACT**
   Bracts are tiny leaves that are often attached around a node.

9. **OPPOSITE LEAF ARRANGEMENT**
   In this arrangement, two leaves share the same node and are positioned opposite each other on the stem (see page 213).

10. **ALTERNATING LEAF ARRANGEMENT**
    In this arrangement, each leaf has its own node and bract(s) (see page 213).

NOTE

Leaves in both the opposite and alternate arrangements can be distributed in a row or spiral around the main stem or vine.

Flowers

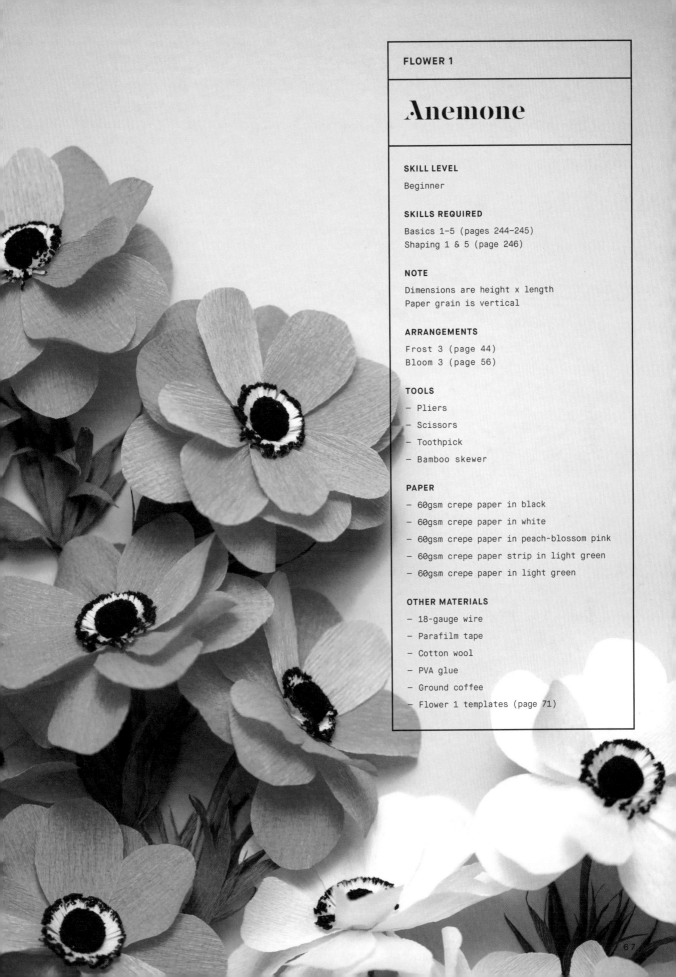

Anemone

SKILL LEVEL
Beginner

SKILLS REQUIRED
Basics 1–5 (pages 244–245)
Shaping 1 & 5 (page 246)

NOTE
Dimensions are height x length
Paper grain is vertical

ARRANGEMENTS
Frost 3 (page 44)
Bloom 3 (page 56)

TOOLS
– Pliers
– Scissors
– Toothpick
– Bamboo skewer

PAPER
– 60gsm crepe paper in black
– 60gsm crepe paper in white
– 60gsm crepe paper in peach-blossom pink
– 60gsm crepe paper strip in light green
– 60gsm crepe paper in light green

OTHER MATERIALS
– 18-gauge wire
– Parafilm tape
– Cotton wool
– PVA glue
– Ground coffee
– Flower 1 templates (page 71)

Stem

1. Cut three pieces of wire, each 25 cm (10 in) long. Bunch them together, then wrap the entire length of the stem with parafilm tape.

Centre

2. Cut one 4 x 4 cm (1½ x 1½ in) square of black paper.

3. Put a small amount of cotton wool around one end of the stem to form a ball. Cover the cotton wool ball with the black paper square and use parafilm tape to secure the paper to the stem.

4. Using a toothpick, cover the surface of the covered cotton wool ball with a small amount of PVA glue, then dip it into ground coffee to cover. Allow to dry.

Stamens

5. Cut a 2.5 x 18 cm (1 x 7 in) piece of white paper and fringe the top 1.5 cm (½ in). Wrap the unfringed section of the paper around the base of the flower centre and secure with PVA glue.

6. Holding the stem, lightly dip the tips of the fringe into PVA glue and then into ground coffee. Tap off any excess coffee, then allow to dry.

Petals

7. Using peach-blossom pink paper, cut three small petals with template A, three medium petals with template B, and seven large petals with template C. Use the edge cut-out technique on a few of the petals.

8. Layer 1: Using PVA glue, attach the bottom 1 cm (½ in) of two A petals and one B petal evenly around the base of the flower centre.

9. Layer 2: Attach two B petals and one C petal around the base of layer 1, between the gaps of the attached petals.

10. Layer 3: Attach the remaining petals randomly around the base of the flower centre.

11. Starting from the base of the flower, wrap the entire length of the stem with light-green paper strip, securing with PVA glue.

Leaves

12. Using the light-green paper, cut five leaves with template D. Scrunch and twist all the leaves. Use PVA glue to attach the leaves evenly around the stem, 7–10 cm (2¾–4 in) below the base of the flower.

13. Wrap the stem with another layer of light-green paper, starting from the base of the leaves.

14. Using a bamboo skewer, curl several leaves outwards and away from the stem.

Finishing

15. Gently bend the stem to create a natural shape.

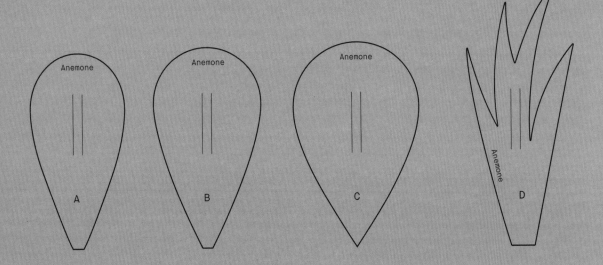

Anemone

A

Anemone

B

Anemone

C

Anemone

D

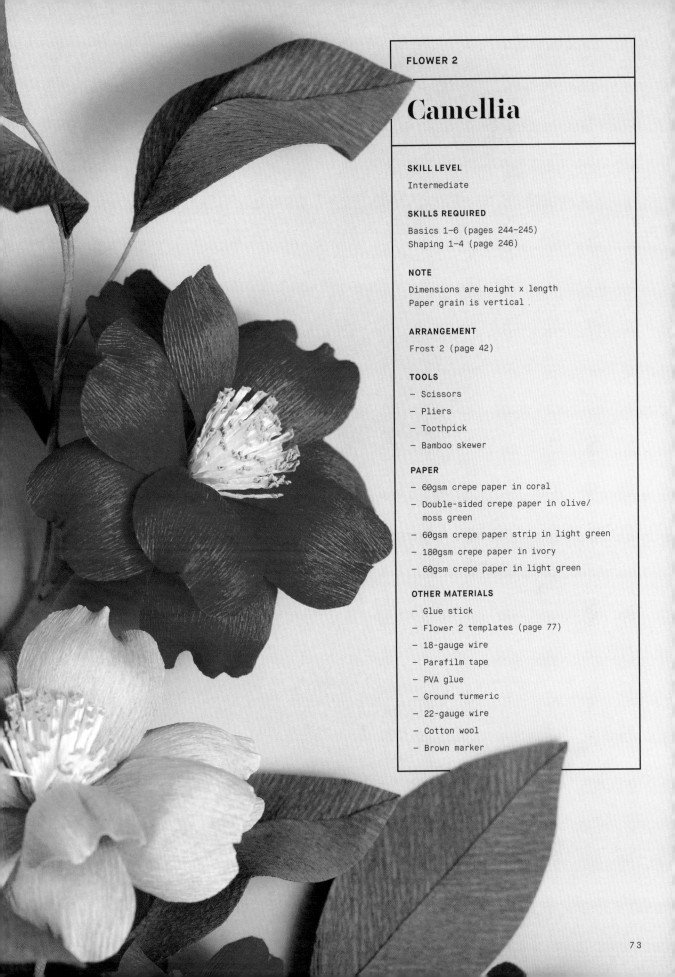

FLOWER 2

Camellia

SKILL LEVEL
Intermediate

SKILLS REQUIRED
Basics 1–6 (pages 244–245)
Shaping 1–4 (page 246)

NOTE
Dimensions are height x length
Paper grain is vertical .

ARRANGEMENT
Frost 2 (page 42)

TOOLS
- Scissors
- Pliers
- Toothpick
- Bamboo skewer

PAPER
- 60gsm crepe paper in coral
- Double-sided crepe paper in olive/
  moss green
- 60gsm crepe paper strip in light green
- 180gsm crepe paper in ivory
- 60gsm crepe paper in light green

OTHER MATERIALS
- Glue stick
- Flower 2 templates (page 77)
- 18-gauge wire
- Parafilm tape
- PVA glue
- Ground turmeric
- 22-gauge wire
- Cotton wool
- Brown marker

Preparation

1. Cut two 50 x 15 cm (20 x 6 in) pieces of coral paper. Paste the sheets together using the glue stick. Allow to dry.

2. Using the olive/moss-green double-sided paper and following the Basic Leaf method (page 219, steps 2–8), make three leaves with template A and five leaves with template B.

Stem

3. Cut three pieces of 18-gauge wire, each 25 cm (10 in) long. Bunch them together and wrap the entire length of the stem with parafilm tape. Wrap the stem with light-green paper strip, securing with PVA glue.

Centre

4. Cut a 4 x 12 cm (1½ x 4¾ in) strip of ivory paper and fringe the top 3 cm (1¼ in). Wrap the unfringed section around one end of the stem and secure with PVA glue.

5. Trim the paper to even the fringe.

6. Holding the stem, lightly dip the tips of the fringe into PVA glue and then into ground turmeric. Shake off any excess turmeric, then allow to dry.

Petals

7. Using the pasted coral sheet, cut ten petals with template C. Curl, cup and ruffle the edges of all the petals.

8. Layer 1: Using PVA glue, attach three petals evenly around the base of the flower centre.

9. Layer 2: Attach the remaining petals around the base of the layer 1, between the gaps of the attached petals.

10. Cover the base of the flower with light-green paper strip.

Leaves

11. Cut three pieces of 22-gauge wire, each 15 cm (6 in) long. Wrap the entire length of each stem with light-green paper strip, securing with PVA glue.

12. Using PVA glue, attach one A leaf to the main flower stem, about 1 cm (½ in) below the base of the flower. Attach two B leaves next to it, so that the leaves are evenly distributed around the flower. Cover the base of the leaves with light-green paper strip.

13. Working with the remaining B leaves and the short wires, adhere the top 3 cm (1¼ in) of each wire to the back of a leaf. Using PVA glue, join the stems together, leaving 1 cm (½ in) between the base of each leaf and the node. Cover the join with light-green paper strip.

14. Using PVA glue, attach the bottom 11 cm (4¼ in) of the sprig of leaves to the main flower stem, 13 cm (5 in) below the base of the flower. Cover the join with light-green paper strip.

$\longrightarrow$

Buds

15. Cut a 35 cm (14 in) piece of 22-gauge wire. Wrap the entire length of the stem with light-green paper strip, securing with PVA glue.

16. Cut a 4 x 4 cm (1½ x 1½ in) square of coral paper, then fold it in half across the diagonal.

17. Make a small cotton wool ball and put it in the fold of the paper. Fold the left and right corners down to meet the bottom corner, so that the cotton wool is covered. When you finish, your bud should have a pointy top. Gently pinch the base of the bud.

18. Attach the base of the bud to one end of the stem using parafilm tape, then cover the base with light-green paper strip.

19. Using light-green paper, cut three sepals with template D. Use brown marker to colour the edges.

20. Using PVA glue, attach the sepals evenly around the bottom half of the bud. Cover the base of the bud with light-green paper strip.

21. Repeat steps 15–20 to make two more buds.

22. Using PVA glue, join the bud stems together along their whole length. Wrap the stem with light-green paper strip.

23. Attach the remaining two A leaves below the base of the buds using PVA glue. Cover the leaf joints with light-green paper strip.

Assembly

24. Using PVA glue, attach the bottom 11 cm (4¼ in) of the sprig of buds to the flower stem, 13 cm (5 in) below the base of the flower. Cover the join with light-green paper strip.

Finishing

25. Gently bend the flower stem to create a natural look.

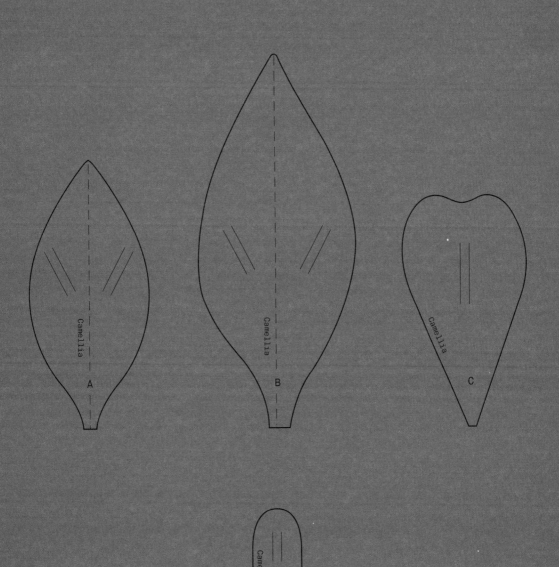

Camellia A

Camellia B

Camellia C

Camellia D

Chrysanthemum

SKILL LEVEL

Intermediate

SKILLS REQUIRED

Basics 1, 2, 3 & 5 (pages 244–245)
Shaping 1 & 3 (page 246)

NOTE

Dimensions are height x length
Paper grain is vertical

ARRANGEMENT

Harvest 5 (page 36)

TOOLS

- Pliers
- Scissors
- Toothpick
- Scallop edgers
- Bamboo skewer

PAPER

- 60gsm crepe paper strip in light green
- 180gsm crepe paper in plum
- 180gsm crepe paper strip in ivy green
- Double-sided crepe paper in olive/
  moss green

OTHER MATERIALS

- 18-gauge wire
- Parafilm tape
- PVA glue
- Cotton wool
- Flower 3 templates (page 83)

Stem

1. Cut three pieces of 18-gauge wire, each 30 cm (12 in) long. Bunch them together and wrap the entire length of the stem with parafilm tape. Wrap the stem with light-green paper strip, securing with PVA glue.

Centre

2. Cut one 5 x 2 cm (2 x ¾ in) rectangle of plum paper. Gently stretch the piece of paper crosswise to make it into a square.

3. Put a small amount of cotton wool around one end of the stem to form a ball. Cover the cotton wool ball with the plum paper square. Use parafilm tape to secure the paper to the stem, then cover the tape with light-green paper strip.

Petals

4. Layers 1 & 2: Cut two 3 x 15 cm (1¼ x 6 in) strips of plum paper. Use scallop edgers to trim the top edge of each strip. Fringe the top 2 cm (¾ in) of each strip to separate the scallops, then curl the fringe with a bamboo skewer.

5. Using a toothpick, dab a small amount of PVA glue around the base of the flower centre, then wrap the unfringed edge of the first plum strip around the base. Make sure that the fringe is curling inwards and apply more glue as you go to make sure that the paper is firmly attached to the base.

6. Glue some of the petals to the flower centre, so that it is completely covered.

7. Wrap the unfringed edge of the second plum paper strip around the base of the flower, again with the fringe curling inward. Secure with PVA glue.

8. Layers 3 & 4: Cut two 4 x 15 cm (1½ x 6 in) strips of plum paper. Use scallop edgers to trim the top edge of each strip. Fringe the top 3 cm (1¼ in) of each strip to separate the scallops, then curl the fringe. One at a time, wrap the unfringed edge of each strip around the base of the flower, securing with PVA glue.

9. Layers 5 & 6: Cut two 6 x 15 cm (2½ x 6 in) strips of plum paper. Use scallop edgers to trim the top edge of each strip. Fringe the top 4.5 cm (1¾ in) of each strip to separate the scallops, then curl the fringe. One at a time, wrap the unfringed edge of each strip around the base of the flower, securing with PVA glue.

10. Layers 7, 8 & 9: Cut three 8 x 15 cm (3¼ x 6 in) strips of plum paper. Use scallop edgers to trim the top edge of each strip. Fringe the top 6 cm (2½ in) of each strip to separate the scallops, then curl the fringe. One at a time, wrap the unfringed edge of each strip around the base of the flower, securing with PVA glue.

11. Starting from the base of the flower, wrap ivy-green paper strip around the entire stem to thicken it. Secure with PVA glue.

12. Again starting from the base of the flower, wrap light-green paper strip around the entire stem to cover the ivy-green paper. Secure with PVA glue.

$\longrightarrow$

Leaves

13. Using the olive/moss-green double-sided paper and following the Basic Leaf method (page 219, steps 2–8), make one leaf with template A and one leaf with template B. In step 2 of the Basic Leaf method, change the dimensions of the double-sided paper to 24 x 12 cm (9½ x 4¾ in).

14. Using PVA glue, attach the large leaf to the stem, 15 cm (6 in) below the base of the flower. Cover the leaf joint with light-green paper strip.

15. Attach the small leaf to the stem, about 2 cm (¾ in) below the large leaf. Cover the leaf joint with light-green paper strip.

Finishing

16. Bend the petals outwards to open the flower.

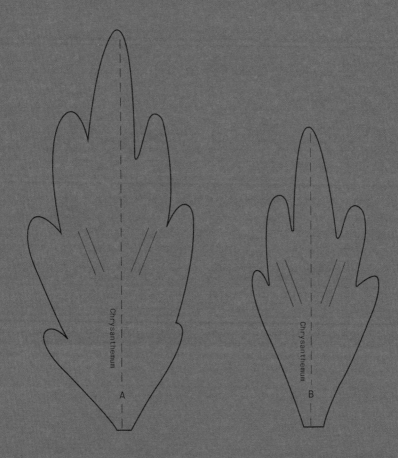

Chrysanthemum A

Chrysanthemum B

Clematis

SKILL LEVEL

Beginner

SKILLS REQUIRED

Basics 1, 4 & 5 (pages 244–245)
Shaping 1–3 (page 246)

NOTE

Dimensions are height x length
Paper grain is vertical

ARRANGEMENTS

Sunshine 2 (page 18)
Harvest 5 (page 36)

TOOLS

– Pliers
– Toothpick
– Scissors
– Bamboo skewer

PAPER

– 60gsm crepe paper strip in light green
– 180gsm crepe paper in lime pulp
– Double-sided crepe paper in olive/
  moss green
– 60gsm crepe paper in fuchsia

OTHER MATERIALS

– 18-gauge wire
– PVA glue
– 22-gauge wire
– Flower 4 templates (page 89)

Flowersmith — Flowers

Vine

1. Cut one 40 cm (16 in) piece of 18-gauge wire. Wrap the entire length of the vine with light-green paper strip, securing with PVA glue.

Flower

PART 1

2. Cut one 15 cm (6 in) piece of 22-gauge wire. Wrap the entire length of the stem with light-green paper strip, securing with PVA glue.

3. Cut one 2 x 3 cm (¾ x 1¼ in) piece of lime-pulp paper. Gently stretch the piece of paper crosswise to increase the width to 6 cm (2½ in). Fringe the top 1.5 cm (½ in) of the rectangle.

4. Wrap the unfringed edge of the paper around one end of the stem, securing with PVA glue.

5. Using olive/moss-green double-sided paper, cut two small leaves with template A. Slightly twist the top 1 cm (½ in) of each leaf.

6. Using PVA glue, attach the leaves to the stem, 3 cm (1¼ in) below the base of the fringed centre. Cover the leaf joints with light-green paper.

7. Gently curl the leaves with a bamboo skewer. Bend the stem to create a natural look.

8. Repeat steps 2–4 to make a second stem and centre, without leaves. This will be used for part 2.

PART 2

9. Using fuchsia paper, cut four petals with template B.

10. Cup each petal, curl the top edge outwards, then create a fold down the middle.

11. Pinch the bottom 1 cm (½ in) of each petal, then attach them evenly around the base of the second centre using PVA glue. Cover the base of the flower with light-green paper strip. Join the stem made in part 1 to this flower stem, 3 cm (1¼ in) below the flower and 5 cm (2 in) below the leaves. Cover the join with light-green paper strip.

PART 3

12. Cut two pieces of 22-gauge wire, each 15 cm (6 in) long. Wrap the entire length of each stem with light-green paper strip, securing with PVA glue.

13. Using olive/moss-green double-sided paper and following the Basic Leaf method (page 219, steps 2–8), make two leaves with template C.

14. Using PVA glue, adhere the top 3 cm (1¼ in) of one stem to the back of a leaf. Repeat with the other stem and leaf.

15. Using PVA glue, join the two leaf stems together, leaving 1 cm (½ in) between the base of each leaf and the node. Cover the join with light-green paper strip.

16. Attach this leaf stem to the sprig made in part 2, about 5 cm (2 in) below the node.

17. Repeat steps 2–16 to make two more finished flower sprigs.

Assembly

18. Using PVA glue, attach one finished flower sprig firmly to the end of the main vine, so that the top end of the vine meets the leaf join. Cover the join with light-green paper strip. Attach the remaining two sprigs to the vine, about 6 cm (2½ in) apart. Cover the joins with light-green paper strip.

Finishing

19. Add extra wires to strengthen the vine if required.

NOTE

Add more branches if you wish to extend the vine.

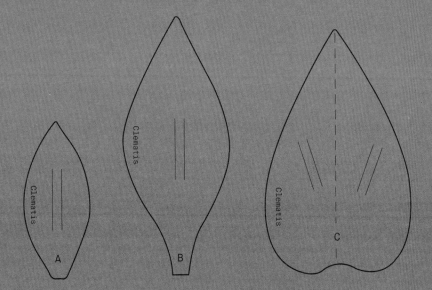

A

Clematis

B

Clematis

C

Clematis

Cosmos

SKILL LEVEL

Beginner

SKILLS REQUIRED

Basics 1, 4 & 5 (pages 244–245)
Shaping 1 & 4 (page 246)
Colouring 1 & 2 (page 247)

NOTE

Dimensions are height x length
Paper grain is vertical

ARRANGEMENTS

Sunshine 3 (page 20)
Sunshine 4 (page 22)
Frost 5 (page 48)

TOOLS

- Scissors
- Flat paintbrush (optional)
- Pliers
- Toothpick
- Bamboo skewer

PAPER

- 60gsm crepe paper in sweet pea
- 60gsm crepe paper strip in light green
- 60gsm crepe paper in yellow
- 60gsm crepe paper in light green

OTHER MATERIALS

- Flower 5 templates (page 95)
- Pink marker or red food dye
- 16-gauge wire
- PVA glue
- Brown marker

Flowersmith — Flowers

Preparation

1. Using sweet-pea paper, cut seven petals with template A.

2. Colour the tips of each petal pink. You can do this using either the edge drawing technique with the pink marker, or using the wet-wash technique with the red food dye and flat paintbrush. Allow the ink/dye to dry completely.

Stem

3. Cut one 30 cm (12 in) piece of 16-gauge wire. Wrap the entire length of the stem with light-green paper strip, securing with PVA glue.

Centre

4. Cut a 2 x 10 cm (¾ x 4 in) strip of yellow paper. Gently stretch the piece of paper crosswise to increase the width to about 15 cm (6 in).

5. Use the brown marker to colour the bottom 1.5 cm (½ in) of the yellow paper strip. Once the ink has dried, finely fringe the top 1 cm (½ in) of the strip.

6. Fold the fringed paper in half four times, until it resembles a tassel. Gently twist the fringe back and forth several times, then unwrap the paper strip completely.

7. Wrap the unfringed edge of the paper strip around one end of the stem, securing with PVA glue.

Petals

8. Curl and ruffle the edges of the pink petals you prepared earlier. Pinch together the bottom 1 cm (½ in) of each petal.

9. Attach the petals evenly around the base of the flower centre using PVA glue.

Calyx

10. Using light-green paper, cut one calyx with template B.

11. Twist and curl the individual sepals.

12. Wrap the calyx around the stem, 5 mm (¼ in) below the base of the flower, so that the sepals are evenly distributed. Secure with PVA glue.

Finishing

13. Gently bend the stem to create a natural look.

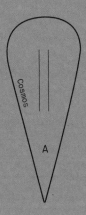

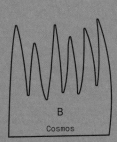

Daffodil

SKILL LEVEL
Beginner

SKILLS REQUIRED
Basics 1–5 (pages 244–245)
Shaping 1 & 4 (page 246)

NOTE
Dimensions are height x length
Paper grain is vertical

ARRANGEMENT
Frost 1 (page 40)

TOOLS

– Scissors

– Toothpick

– Pliers

– Bamboo skewer

PAPER

– 60gsm crepe paper in vanilla

– 180gsm crepe paper strip in ivy green

– 60gsm crepe paper strip in dark green

– 60gsm crepe paper in dark green

OTHER MATERIALS

– PVA glue

– 18-gauge wire

– Parafilm tape in white

– Double-headed artificial stamens in white or pearl

– Flower 6 templates (page 101)

Preparation

1. Cut one 5 x 9 cm (2 x 3½ in) piece of vanilla paper.

2. Using PVA glue, paste the two vertical edges of the paper together along the grain to form a cylinder. Allow the glue to dry completely.

Stem

3. Cut three pieces of wire, each 20 cm (8 in) long. Bunch them together and wrap the entire length of the stem with parafilm tape.

Stamens

4. Cut two double-headed stamens in half, then attach three heads onto one end of the stem using parafilm tape.

Corona

5. Take the vanilla cylinder you made earlier and ruffle the top edge of the paper. Then gently pinch the bottom of the cylinder together. Holding the pinched end with one hand, press your other thumb against the inside of the cylinder to form a cup shape.

6. Slide the bottom of the stem through the cup opening. Using parafilm tape, secure the pinched end of the corona to the stem, 3 cm (1¼ in) below the stamens.

Petals

7. Using vanilla paper, cut six petals with template A. Ruffle the top edges and create a fold down the middle of each petal.

8. Layer 1: Using parafilm tape, attach the bottom 1 cm (½ in) of three petals evenly around the base of the corona.

9. Layer 2: Attach the remaining petals around the base of layer 1, between the gaps of the attached petals.

10. Wrap the entire stem with ivy-green paper strip to thicken it, securing with PVA glue. Repeat using dark-green paper strip.

Spathe

11. Using dark-green paper, cut one spathe with template B.

12. Using PVA glue, attach the spathe to the stem, about 5 cm (2 in) below the base of the flower.

Leaves

13. Using dark-green paper, cut two leaves with template C.

14. Apply a small amount of PVA glue to the bottom 2 cm (¾ in) of one leaf, then wrap it around the bottom 2 cm (¾ in) of the stem, positioning the leaf on the left side of the flower.

15. Using the same method, attach the remaining leaf on the right side of the flower.

Finishing

16. Gently curl the top of each leaf and bend the top of the stem to one side.

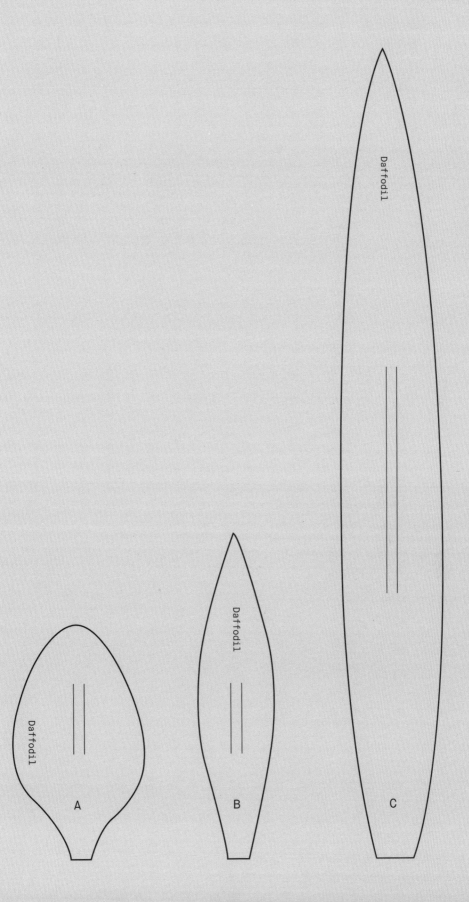

Daffodil

Daffodil

Daffodil

A

B

C

FLOWER 7

Dahlia

SKILL LEVEL

Advanced

SKILLS REQUIRED

Basics 1 & 5 (pages 244–245)
Shaping 1 & 2 (page 246)
Colouring 2 (page 247)

NOTE

Dimensions are height x length
Paper grain is vertical

ARRANGEMENTS

Harvest 1 (page 28)
Harvest 4 (page 34)

TOOLS

— Scissors

— Toothpick

— Pliers

— Bamboo skewer

PAPER

— 60gsm crepe paper in salmon

— 60gsm crepe paper strip in light green

— 60gsm crepe paper in light green

— Double-sided crepe paper in olive/
  moss green

OTHER MATERIALS

— Flower 7 templates (page 107)

— PVA glue

— 18-gauge wire

— Parafilm tape

— Cotton wool

— Red marker

Preparation

1. Using salmon paper, cut nine petals with template A, nine petals with template B and 27 petals with template C. Separate the petals by template.

2. Working with one petal at a time, hold the middle of the petal with your left thumb and index finger. Then, using your right thumb and index finger, twist the top 1 cm (½ in) of the petal. Gently cup each petal after twisting.

3. Dab a small amount of PVA glue on the bottom 1 cm (½ in) of the petal using a toothpick. Fold in the bottom left side of the petal and then the bottom right side, to overlap by 2–3 mm (¹⁄₁₆ in). Gently press the bottom to secure the folds. Allow to dry.

Stem

4. Cut three pieces of 18-gauge wire, each 30 cm (12 in) long. Bunch them together and wrap the entire length of the stem with parafilm tape. Wrap the stem with light-green paper strip, securing with PVA glue.

Centre

5. Cut a 4 x 4 cm (1½ x 1½ in) square of salmon paper, then fold it in half across the diagonal.

6. Make a small cotton wool ball and put it in the fold of the paper. Fold the left and right corners down to meet the bottom corner, so that the cotton wool is covered. When you finish, your bud should have a pointy top. Gently pinch the base of the bud.

7. Attach the base of the bud to one end of the stem using parafilm tape, then cover the base with light-green paper strip.

Petals

8. Layer 1: Cut a 4 x 18 cm (1½ x 7 in) strip of salmon paper. Fold the paper in half four times. Cut out the petal shape using template D, making sure that you do not cut into the dotted lines. Unfold the paper and attach the straight edge of the petal strip around the base of the flower centre using PVA glue. Gently curl the petals inwards. Glue the tips of some petals to the flower centre, so that it is completely covered.

9. Layer 2: Using PVA glue, attach the bottom 1 cm (½ in) of the nine A petals evenly around the base of layer 1.

10. Layer 3: Attach the bottom 1 cm (½ in) of the nine B petals around the base of layer 2, between the gaps of the attached petals.

11. Layer 4: Attach the bottom 1 cm (½ in) of nine C petals around the base of layer 3, between the gaps of the attached petals.

12. Layer 5: Attach the bottom 1 cm (½ in) of nine C petals around the base of layer 4, between the gaps of the attached petals.

13. Layer 6: Attach the bottom 1 cm (½ in) of the remaining nine C petals around the base of layer 5, between the gaps of the attached petals.

Calyx

14. Cut one 4 x 9 cm (1½ x 3½ in) strip of light-green paper. Fold the paper in half three times. Cut a sepal shape using template D, making sure that you do not cut into the dotted lines. Unfold the paper.

15. Wrap the sepal strip (calyx) around the base of the flower, securing with PVA glue. Gently curl the sepals outwards.

Leaves

16. Using olive/moss-green double-sided paper and following the Basic Leaf method (page 219, steps 2–8), make one leaf with template E and one leaf with template F. In step 2 of the Basic Leaf method, change the dimensions of the double-sided paper to 24 x 12 cm (9½ x 4¾ in.)

$\longrightarrow$

Bud

17. Cut three pieces of wire, each 40 cm (16 in) long. Bunch them together and wrap the entire length of the stem with parafilm tape. Wrap the stem with light-green paper strip, securing with PVA glue.

18. Cut one 6 x 6 cm (2½ x 2½ in) square of salmon paper.

19. Put a small amount of cotton wool around one end of the stem to form a ball. Cover the cotton wool ball with the salmon paper square. Use parafilm tape to secure the paper to the stem, then cover the tape with light-green paper strip.

20. Cut one 4 x 9 cm (1½ x 3½ in) strip of light-green paper. Fold the paper in half three times. Cut out the sepal shape using template D, making sure that you do not cut into the dotted lines. Unfold the paper, then use a red marker to colour the edges of the sepals.

21. Wrap the sepal strip around the base of the bud, securing with PVA glue. Glue the bottom two-thirds of each sepal onto the centre. Allow to dry, then curl the tips of the sepals outwards.

Calyx

22. Cut one 4 x 9 cm (1½ x 3½ in) strip of light-green paper. Fold the paper in half three times. Cut out the sepal shape using template D, making sure that you do not cut into the dotted lines.

23. Wrap the sepal strip (calyx) around the base of the bud, securing with PVA glue. Gently curl the sepals outwards.

Assembly

24. Gently bend the stem and bud to create a natural look.

25. Using PVA glue, join the bottom 15 cm (6 in) of the bud stem to the bottom of the main flower stem. Cover the join with light-green paper strip.

26. At the node, attach the two leaves opposite each other using PVA glue. Cover the leaf joints with light-green paper strip.

NOTE

Add more buds and foliage if you wish.

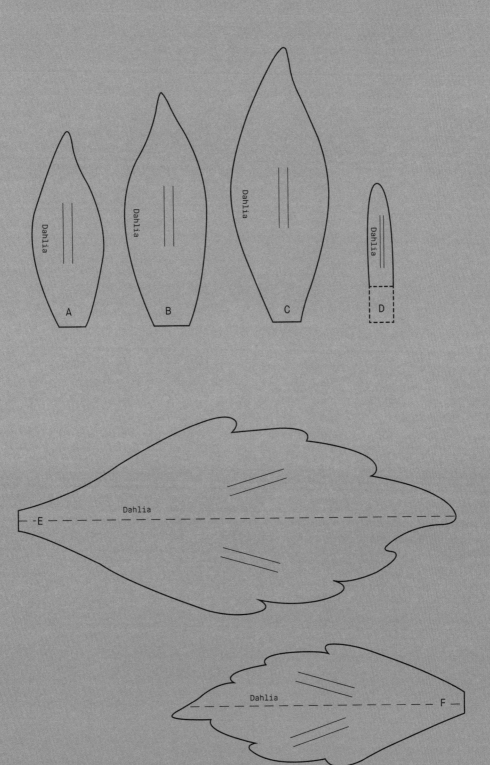

Dahlia

A

Dahlia

B

Dahlia

C

Dahlia

D

Dahlia

-E

Dahlia

F-

Delphinium

SKILL LEVEL
Intermediate

SKILLS REQUIRED
Basics 1, 4 & 5 (pages 244–245)
Shaping 1, 3 & 4 (page 246)

NOTE
Dimensions are height x length
Paper grain is vertical

ARRANGEMENT
Sunshine 3 (page 20)

TOOLS
- Scissors
- Pliers
- Toothpick
- Bamboo skewer

PAPER
- 60gsm crepe paper in light green
- 60gsm crepe paper in white
- 60gsm crepe paper in midnight blue
- 60gsm crepe paper strip in light green

OTHER MATERIALS
- Flower 8 templates (page 113)
- 18-gauge wire
- Parafilm tape
- PVA glue
- 22-gauge wire
- Cotton wool

Preparation

1. Using light-green paper, cut six sepals with template A, 44 bracts with template B and 14 strips measuring 1.5 x 5 cm (½ x 2 in). Fringe the top 1 cm (½ in) of each strip.

2. Using white paper, cut 14 petals using template C and eight 4 x 4 cm (1½ x 1½ in) squares.

3. Using midnight-blue paper, cut 20 petals with template D, 30 petals with template E, 45 petals with template F and 44 petals with template G. (To hasten this process, stack several pieces of paper together before cutting, making sure that the grains are aligned.) Gently ruffle the top edges of the petals.

Stems

4. Cut three pieces of 18-gauge wire, each 40–45 cm (16–18 in) long. Bunch them together and wrap the entire length of the wire with parafilm tape. Wrap the stem with light-green paper strip, securing with PVA glue. This will be the main stem.

5. Cut 22 pieces of 22-gauge wire, each 5 cm (2 in) long. Wrap the entire length of each wire with light-green paper strip. These will be the stems of the buds and florets.

Round buds

6. Put a small amount of cotton wool around one end of a short stem to form a ball. Cover the cotton wool ball with a white paper square. Use parafilm tape to secure the paper to the stem, then cover the tape with light-green paper strip.

7. Glue two sepals onto the bud, then cover the base of the bud with light-green paper strip.

8. Glue two bracts onto the stem, one at the base of the bud and the other just below the base. Gently twist and curl the bracts.

9. Repeat steps 6–8 to make two more round buds.

Cone-shaped buds

10. Fold a white paper square in half across the diagonal. Make a small cotton wool ball and put it in the fold of the paper. Fold the left and right corners down to meet the bottom corner, so that the cotton wool is covered. When you finish, your bud should have a pointy top. Pinch the base of the bud, then attach it to one end of a short stem using parafilm tape.

11. Use PVA glue to attach four D petals evenly around the bud, then cover the base of the bud with light-green paper strip.

12. Glue the tips of the petals to the centre of the bud so that it is almost completely covered.

13. Using PVA glue, attach two bracts to the stem, one at the base of the bud and the other just below the base. Gently twist and curl the bracts.

14. Repeat steps 10–13 to make four more cone-shaped buds.

Small florets

15. Wrap a fringed paper strip around one end of a short stem, securing the straight edge to the stem using PVA glue.

16. Wrap one C petal evenly around the fringed centre, securing with PVA glue.

17. Attach six E petals around the base of the flower.

18. Attach two bracts to the stem, one at the base of the flower and the other 1 cm (½ in) below the base. Gently twist and curl the bracts.

19. Repeat steps 15–18 to make four more small florets.

→

Medium florets

20. Wrap a fringed paper strip around one end of a short stem, securing the straight edge to the stem using PVA glue.

21. Wrap one C petal evenly around the fringed centre, securing with PVA glue.

22. Attach nine F petals around the base of the flower.

23. Attach two bracts to the stem, one at the base of the flower and the other 1 cm (½ in) below the base. Gently twist and curl the bracts.

24. Repeat steps 20–23 to make four more medium florets.

Large florets

25. Wrap a fringed paper strip around one end of a short stem, securing the straight edge to the stem using PVA glue.

26. Wrap one C petal evenly around the fringed centre, securing with PVA glue.

27. Attach 11 of the G petals around the base of the flower.

28. Attach two bracts to the stem, one at the base of the flower and the other 1 cm (½ in) below the base. Gently twist and curl the bracts.

29. Repeat steps 25–28 to make three more large florets.

Assembly

30. Gently bend the heads of the buds and florets. Using PVA glue, attach all of the buds to the main stem — attach the round buds first, then the cone-shaped buds, working in a downwards spiral and leaving 1–2 cm (½–¾ in) between each bud. Still working in a downwards spiral, attach the small florets, then the medium florets and then the large florets, leaving 3–5 cm (1¼–2 in) between each floret. Make sure to leave 1–2 cm (½–¾ in) between the base of each bud/floret and the point where its stem joins the main stem. Cover the joins with light-green paper strip.

31. Using parafilm tape, add additional wire below the last floret to stabilise the main stem, then cover with light-green paper strip.

Finishing

32. Gently bend the buds and florets to create a natural look.

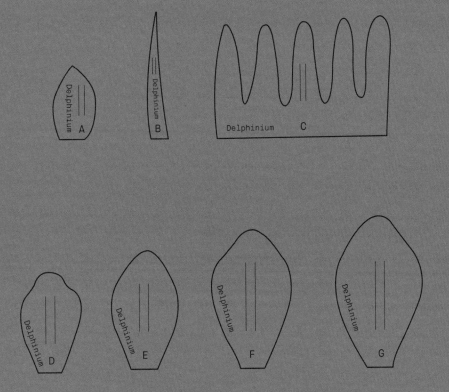

Dogwood

SKILL LEVEL
Beginner

SKILLS REQUIRED
Basics 2, 4 & 5 (pages 244–245)
Shaping 1, 3 & 4 (page 246)
Colouring 1 & 2 (page 247)

NOTE
Dimensions are height x length
Paper grain is vertical

ARRANGEMENT
Bloom 3 (page 56)

TOOLS

– Scissors

– Fan paintbrush

– Pliers

– Toothpick

– Bamboo skewer

PAPER

– 60gsm crepe paper in white

– 60gsm crepe paper strip in dark brown

– 60gsm crepe paper in light green

OTHER MATERIALS

– ½ teaspoon rose-pink food dye

– 2 teaspoons water

– 18-gauge wire

– PVA glue

– 22-gauge wire

– Ground turmeric

– Flower 9 templates (page 119)

– Brown marker

Preparation

1. Cut four 6 x 15 cm (2½ x 6 in) strips of white paper.

2. Dilute the rose-pink food dye in the water. Use the dry-wash technique to colour the top two-thirds of each strip of paper. Allow to dry.

Branch & stems

3. Cut one 30 cm (12 in) piece of 18-gauge wire. Wrap the entire length of the wire with dark-brown paper strip, securing with PVA glue. This will be the main branch.

4. Cut four pieces of 22-gauge wire, each 15 cm (6 in) long. Wrap the entire length of each wire with dark-brown paper strip, securing with PVA glue. These will be the flower stems.

Centres

5. Cut four 1.5 x 5 cm (½ x 2 in) strips of light-green paper. Fringe the top 1 cm (½ in) of each strip.

6. Wrap a fringed paper strip evenly around one end of a short stem, securing the straight edge to the stem using PVA glue.

7. Lightly dip the tips of the fringe into PVA glue, then into ground turmeric. Shake off any excess turmeric, then allow to dry.

8. Repeat steps 5–7 to make three more flower centres.

Petals

9. Using the painted paper strips, cut 16 petals with template A, making sure that the top of the template aligns with the painted edge of the paper.

10. Colour around the edge of the top notch on each petal with brown marker.

11. Curl all the petals.

12. Using PVA glue, attach four petals evenly around a flower centre. Cover the base of the flower with dark-brown paper strip.

13. Repeat steps 9–12 to make three more flowers.

Bracts

14. Using light-green paper, cut two bracts with template B.

15. Using PVA glue, attach one bract to a flower stem, 5 cm (2 in) below the base of the flower. Cover the base of the bract with dark-brown paper strip.

16. Attach the remaining bract to another flower, 3 cm (1¼ in) below the base of the flower. Cover the base of the bract with dark-brown paper strip.

Assembly

17. Using PVA glue, attach the bottom 2 cm (¾ in) of a flower stem to the top end of the main branch. Cover the join with dark-brown paper strip.

18. Below the first join, attach a second flower stem to the branch, leaving 2–3 cm (¾–1¼ in) between the base of this flower and the branch.

19. Attach a third flower stem to the branch, 8–10 cm (3¼–4 in) below the second flower, leaving 4–5 cm (1½–2 in) between the base of this flower and the branch.

20. At the lower node, attach the remaining flower stem to the opposite side of the branch, leaving about 10 cm (4 in) between the base of this flower and the branch.

21. To stabilise the branch, use parafilm tape to add more wire below the last flower. Cover all the joins with dark-brown paper strip.

Finishing

22. Gently bend the branch and stems to create a natural look.

NOTE

Join several branches together to make a larger branch.

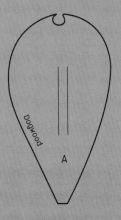

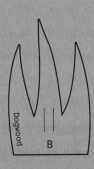

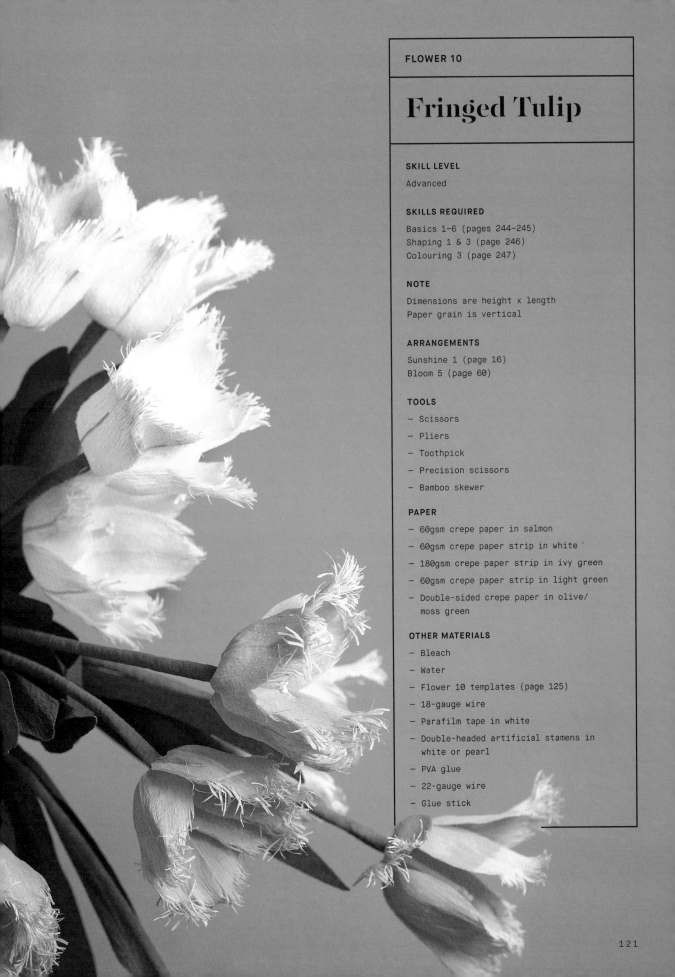

Fringed Tulip

SKILL LEVEL

Advanced

SKILLS REQUIRED

Basics 1–6 (pages 244–245)
Shaping 1 & 3 (page 246)
Colouring 3 (page 247)

NOTE

Dimensions are height x length
Paper grain is vertical

ARRANGEMENTS

Sunshine 1 (page 16)
Bloom 5 (page 60)

TOOLS

– Scissors

– Pliers

– Toothpick

– Precision scissors

– Bamboo skewer

PAPER

– 60gsm crepe paper in salmon

– 60gsm crepe paper strip in white

– 180gsm crepe paper strip in ivy green

– 60gsm crepe paper strip in light green

– Double-sided crepe paper in olive/
  moss green

OTHER MATERIALS

– Bleach

– Water

– Flower 10 templates (page 125)

– 18-gauge wire

– Parafilm tape in white

– Double-headed artificial stamens in
  white or pearl

– PVA glue

– 22-gauge wire

– Glue stick

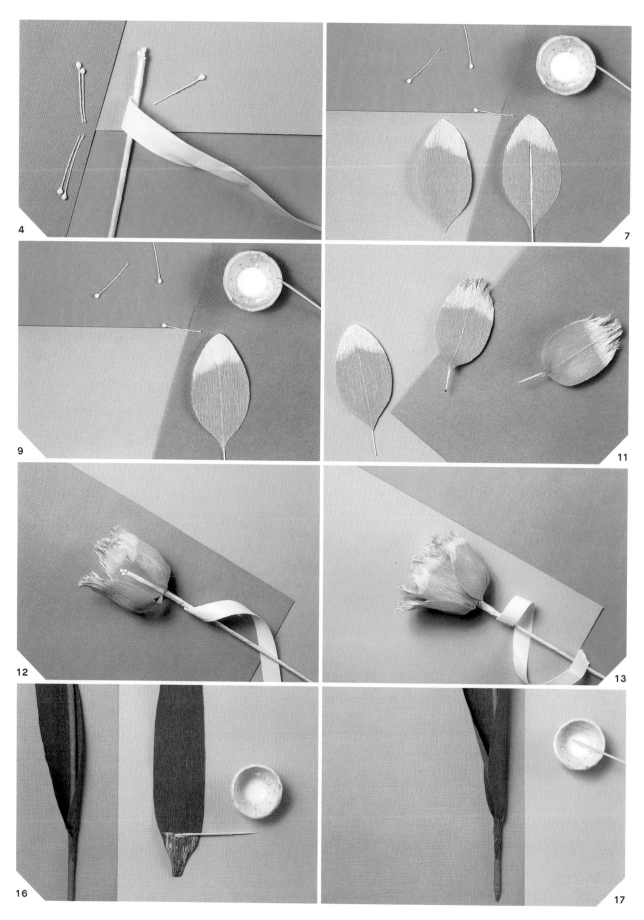

Flowersmith — Flowers

Preparation

1. Cut two strips of salmon paper, each 8 x 30 cm (3 x 12 in), ensuring the grain runs vertically with the short edge. Bleach the top 2 cm (¾ in) of the long edge of each strip. Allow to dry.

2. Cut 12 petals using template A. Make sure that the bleached edges align with the top of the template.

Stem

3. Cut three pieces of 18-gauge wire, each 30 cm (12 in) long. Bunch them together and wrap the entire length of the stem with parafilm tape.

Centre

4. Cut two double-headed stamens in half, then attach three heads onto one end of the stem using parafilm tape.

Petals

5. Cut six pieces of 22-gauge wire, each 7 cm (2¾ in) long. Wrap the entire length of each wire with white paper strip, securing with PVA glue.

6. Put one petal on a flat surface, with the bottom (pointy) end closest to your body. Using a toothpick, dab a small amount of PVA glue down the centre spine of the petal, starting about 1.5 cm (½ in) below the tip.

7. Place a short piece of wire onto the glue on the spine of the petal. Apply pressure to secure the wire to the petal.

8. Using a glue stick, apply a small amount of glue to the surface of the petal, excluding the top 1.5 cm (½ in). Use a minimal amount of glue, to avoid discolouration.

9. Take another petal and place it on top of the first petal, making sure that the two petals align perfectly. Gently press down with your thumb to join the petals together.

10. Repeat steps 5–9 with the remaining petals and short wires, to make five more finished petals. Allow to dry.

11. Use precision scissors to finely fringe the top 1 cm (½ in) of each petal. Bend and gently cup the bottom of each petal.

12. Layer 1: Using parafilm tape, attach three petals to the main stem, 2.5 cm (1 in) below the stamen heads. Make sure the petals are evenly distributed around the flower centre.

13. Layer 2: Attach the remaining three petals around the base of layer 1, between the gaps of the attached petals.

14. Wrap the stem with ivy-green paper strip to thicken the thin section, until the length of the stem is even. Wrap the stem with another layer of ivy-green paper strip, then wrap with light-green paper strip, securing each layer with PVA glue.

Leaves

15. Using olive/moss-green double-sided paper, cut two leaves with template B.

16. Apply PVA glue to the bottom 3 cm (1¼ in) of one leaf, then attach it to the flower stem, approximately 5 cm (2 in) from the bottom of the stem.

17. Attach the remaining leaf 1 cm (½ in) below the first leaf.

18. Curl the leaves to create a natural look.

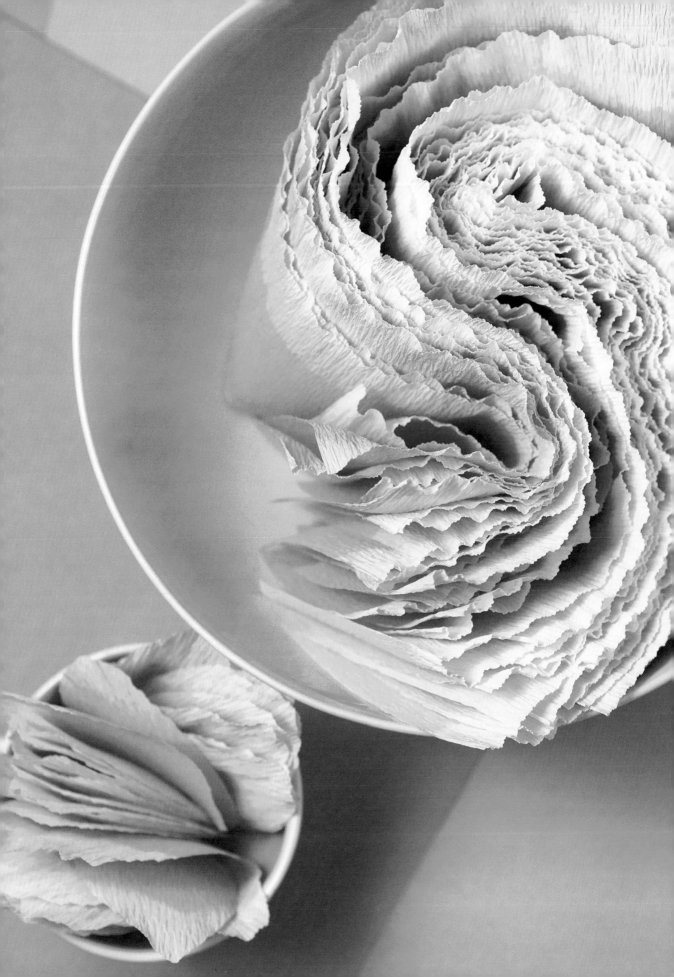

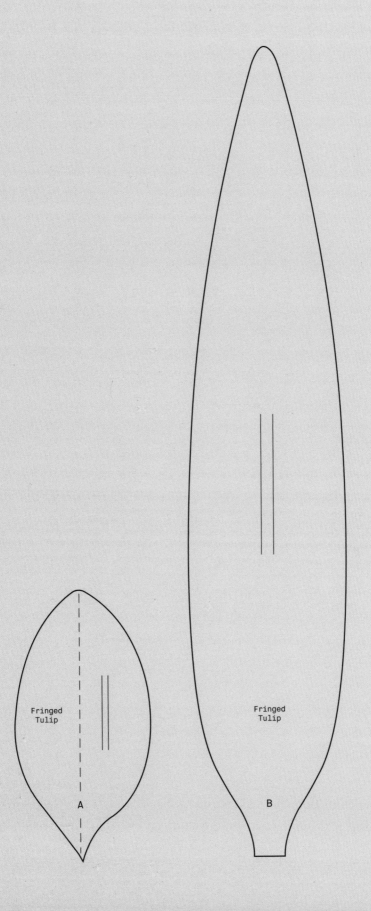

Fringed
Tulip

A

Fringed
Tulip

B

Gardenia

SKILL LEVEL

Intermediate

SKILLS REQUIRED

Basics 1–6 (pages 244–245)
Shaping 1–4 (page 246)

NOTE

Dimensions are height x length
Paper grain is vertical

ARRANGEMENTS

Sunshine 2 (page 18)
Bloom 1 (page 52)

TOOLS

– Scissors

– Pliers

– Toothpick

– Bamboo skewer

PAPER

– 60gsm crepe paper in white

– 60gsm crepe paper strip in light green

– 60gsm crepe paper in light green

– Double-sided crepe paper in olive/
  moss green

OTHER MATERIALS

– Glue stick

– 18-gauge wire

– Parafilm tape

– PVA glue

– Flower 11 templates (page 131)

– 22-gauge wire

– Cotton wool

Preparation

1. Cut two 50 x 15 cm (20 x 6 in) pieces of white paper. Paste the sheets together using the glue stick. Allow to dry.

Stem

2. Cut three pieces of 18-gauge wire, each 25 cm (10 in) long. Bunch them together and wrap the entire length of the stem with parafilm tape. Wrap the stem with light-green paper strip, securing with PVA glue.

Petals

3. Using the pasted white paper sheet, cut six petals with template A, two petals with template B, two petals with template C and seven petals with template D. Separate the petals by template.

4. Put four A petals aside. Cup and curl the rest of the petals, one at a time, as follows: cup the middle, then curl the top of the petal. For a natural look, curl some petals more than others.

5. Layer 1: Using PVA glue, attach the bottom 1 cm (½ in) of the four uncurled A petals evenly around one end of the stem.

6. Layer 2: Take the two remaining A petals and two B petals, and attach the bottom 1 cm (½ in) of the petals evenly around the base of layer 1. Make sure three cups face towards the centre of the flower and one cup faces away.

7. Layer 3: Take the two C petals and two of the D petals. Attach the bottom 1 cm (½ in) of the petals evenly around the base of layer 2.

8. Layer 4: Take the remaining D petals and attach the bottom 1 cm (½ in) of the petals evenly around the base of layer 3. Make sure one cup faces away from the centre.

Calyx

9. Using light-green paper, cut one calyx with template E. Attach the bottom 1 cm (½ in) of the calyx around the base of the flower using PVA glue. Cover the base of the calyx with light-green paper strip, then curl the sepals outwards.

Leaves

10. Cut six pieces of 22-gauge wire, each 15 cm (6 in) long. Wrap the entire length of each stem with light-green paper strip, securing with PVA glue.

11. Using the olive/moss-green double-sided paper and following the Basic Leaf method (page 219, steps 2–8), make six leaves with template F.

12. Adhere the top 3 cm (1¼ in) of each stem to the back of a leaf using PVA glue.

13. Using PVA glue, join three leaf stems together, leaving 1 cm (½ in) between the base of each leaf and the node. Cover the join with light-green paper strip. Repeat with the remaining three leaves to make another sprig.

14. Using PVA glue, attach the bottom 3 cm (2 in) of the first sprig of leaves to the main flower stem, 13 cm (5 in) below the base of the flower. Cover the join with light-green paper strip.

15. Attach the bottom 7 cm (2¾ in) of the second sprig of leaves to the opposite side of the main stem, 2 cm (¾ in) below the first sprig. Cover the join with light-green paper strip.

$\longrightarrow$

Bud

16. Cut one 30 cm (12 in) piece of 18-gauge wire. Wrap the entire length of the stem with light-green paper strip, securing with PVA glue.

17. Cut a 4 x 4 cm (1½ x 1½ in) square of light-green paper, then fold it in half across the diagonal.

18. Make a small cotton wool ball and put it in the fold of the paper. Fold the left and right corners down to meet the bottom corner, so that the cotton wool is covered. When you finish, your bud should have a pointy top. Pinch the base of the bud.

19. Attach the base of the bud to one end of the stem using parafilm tape, then cover the base with light-green paper strip.

20. Using light-green paper, cut three sepals with template G.

21. Using PVA glue, attach the bottom 1 cm (½ in) of the sepals evenly around the bud, 1 cm (½ in) below the base of the bud. Apply a small amount of glue to the surface of the bud. Press the sepals against the bud to secure, then twist the tip into a point.

22. Using light-green paper, cut one calyx with template E. Attach the bottom 1 cm (½ in) of the calyx around the base of the bud using PVA glue. Cover the base of the bud with light-green paper strip, then curl the sepals outwards.

23. Using olive/moss-green double-sided paper and following the Basic Leaf method (page 219, steps 2–8), make two leaves with template H.

24. Using PVA glue, attach one leaf to the stem, 5 cm (2 in) below the base of the bud. Cover the leaf joint with light-green paper strip. Attach the second leaf to the other side of the stem, 2 cm (¾ in) below the first leaf. Cover the leaf joint with light-green paper strip.

25. Gently bend the bud stem to create a natural look.

Assembly

26. Using PVA glue, join the bottom 10 cm (4 in) of the bud stem to the bottom of the flower stem. Cover the join with light-green paper strip.

NOTE

Add more buds and foliage if you wish.

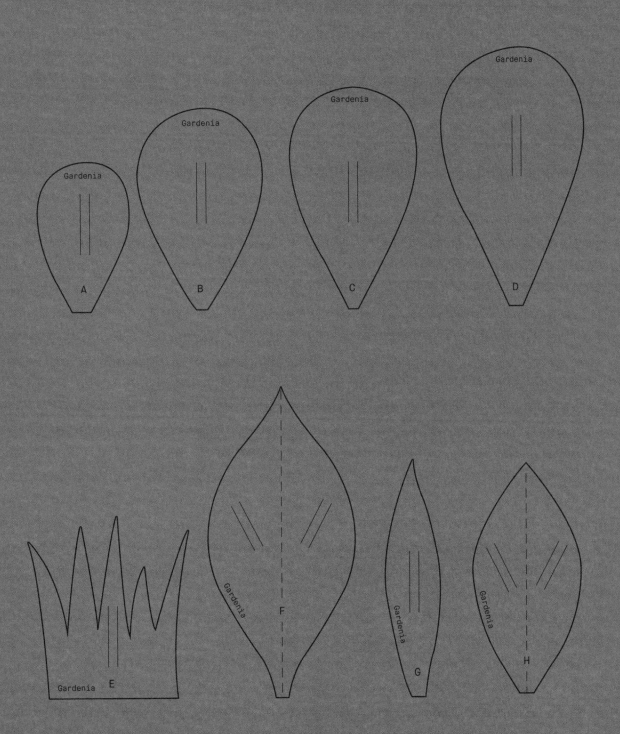

Japanese Anemone

SKILL LEVEL

Beginner

SKILLS REQUIRED

Basics 1–6 (pages 244–245)
Shaping 1, 2, 3 & 5 (page 246)

NOTE

Dimensions are height x length
Paper grain is vertical

ARRANGEMENT

Harvest 4 (page 34)

TOOLS

- Scissors

- Pliers

- Toothpick

- Bamboo skewer

PAPER

- 60gsm crepe paper in white

- 60gsm crepe paper in bubblegum

- 60gsm crepe paper strip in light green

- 60gsm crepe paper in light green

- 60gsm crepe paper in yellow

OTHER MATERIALS

- Flower 12 templates (page 137)

- Glue stick

- 16-gauge wire

- PVA glue

- Cotton wool

- Parafilm tape

- Ground turmeric

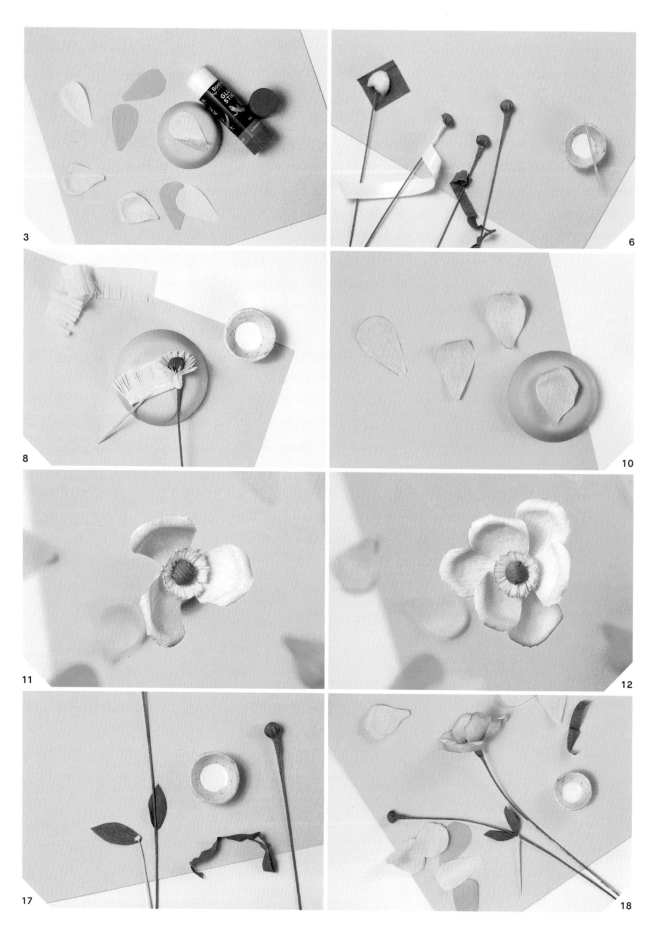

Preparation

1. Using white paper, cut seven petals using template A.

2. Using bubblegum paper, cut seven petals using template A.

3. Using the glue stick, paste together one bubblegum petal and one white petal. Repeat with the remaining petals. Allow to dry.

Stem

4. Cut a 22 cm (8¾ in) piece of wire. Wrap the entire length of the stem with light-green paper strip, securing with PVA glue.

Centre

5. Cut one 3 x 3 cm (1¼ x 1¼ in) square of light-green paper.

6. Put a small amount of cotton wool around one end of the stem to form a ball. Cover the cotton wool ball with the light-green paper square. Use parafilm tape to secure the paper to the stem. Cover the tape with light-green paper strip.

7. Cut one 2 x 15 cm (¾ x 6 in) strip of yellow paper. Gently stretch the piece of paper crosswise to increase the width to 20–25 cm (8–10 in). Fringe the top 1 cm (½ in) of the strip.

8. Wrap the unfringed edge of the paper strip around the base of the flower centre, securing with PVA glue. Trim with scissors to even the fringe.

9. Lightly dip the top of the fringe into PVA glue, then into ground turmeric. Shake off any excess turmeric, then allow to dry.

Petals

10. Cup and curl all the pasted petals. Use the edge cut-out technique on one or two petals.

11. Layer 1: Using PVA glue, attach three petals evenly around the base of the flower centre.

12. Layer 2: Attach the remaining petals around the base of layer 1, between the gaps of the attached petals.

Bud

13. Cut one 25 cm (10 in) piece of 16-gauge wire. Wrap the entire length of the stem with light-green paper strip, securing with PVA glue.

14. Cut one 3 x 3 cm (1¼ x 1¼ in) square of light-green paper.

15. Put a small amount of cotton wool around one end of the stem to form a ball. Cover the cotton wool ball with the light-green paper square. Use parafilm tape to secure the paper to the stem. Cover the tape with light-green paper strip.

16. Using light-green paper, cut two leaves with template B.

17. Using PVA glue, attach the leaves to the stem, 15 cm (6 in) below the base of the bud. Cover the leaf joints with light-green paper strip.

Assembly

18. Using PVA glue, join the bud stem to the flower stem below the leaves, making sure the bottom ends align. Wrap the stem with light-green paper strip.

Finishing

19. Gently bend the stems to create a natural look.

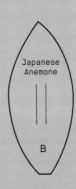

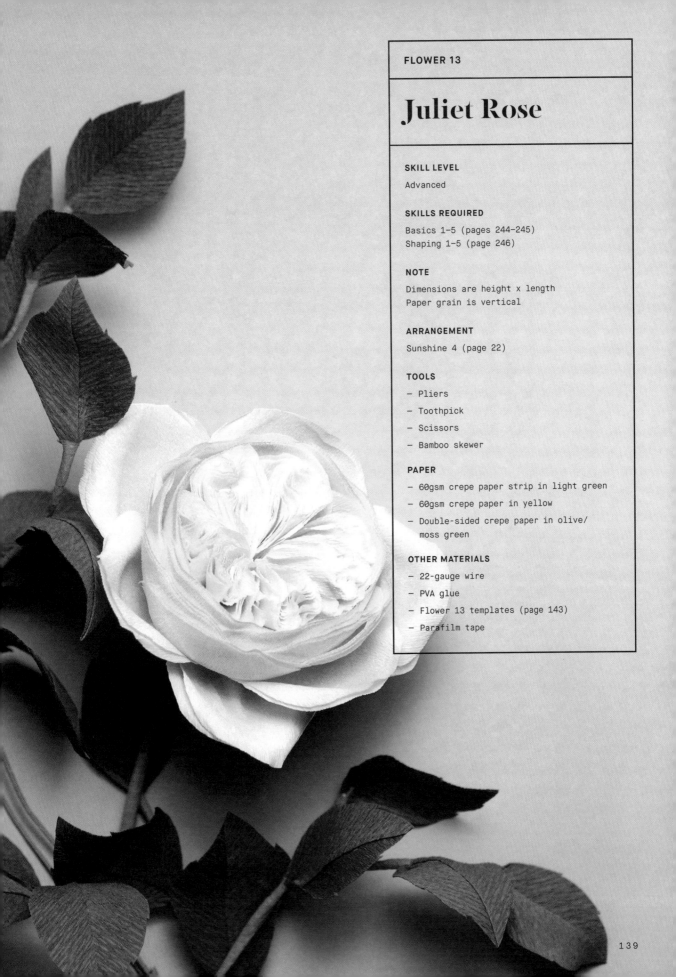

FLOWER 13

Juliet Rose

SKILL LEVEL
Advanced

SKILLS REQUIRED
Basics 1–5 (pages 244–245)
Shaping 1–5 (page 246)

NOTE
Dimensions are height x length
Paper grain is vertical

ARRANGEMENT
Sunshine 4 (page 22)

TOOLS

– Pliers

– Toothpick

– Scissors

– Bamboo skewer

PAPER

– 60gsm crepe paper strip in light green

– 60gsm crepe paper in yellow

– Double-sided crepe paper in olive/
  moss green

OTHER MATERIALS

– 22-gauge wire

– PVA glue

– Flower 13 templates (page 143)

– Parafilm tape

Petals

LAYER 1

1. Cut one 25 cm (10 in) piece of 22-gauge wire. Wrap the entire length of the wire with light-green paper strip, securing with PVA glue.

2. Using yellow paper, cut five petals with template A, four petals with template B and four petals with template C.

3. Gently ruffle the top edge of each petal.

4. Stack the 13 petals on top of each other from biggest to smallest, using PVA glue to paste the bottom 5 mm (¼ in) of the petals together as you go.

5. Using PVA glue, adhere the top 1 cm (½ in) of the stem to the top of the stack of petals. Press firmly to secure the petals to the stem. Allow to dry.

6. Repeat steps 1–5 to make six more petal stacks on wires.

7. Using PVA glue, join the seven finished stems together, 1 cm (¾ in) below the base of the petals, making sure the stacks of petals are evenly distributed so they form a tight cirlce.

8. Gently twist and ruffle the edges of the petals to create a natural look.

LAYER 2

9. Using yellow paper, cut 39 petals with template D and 12 petals with template E. Use the edge cut-out technique on one or two pairs of E petals. Separate the petals by template.

10. Stack three D petals together and cup. Using parafilm tape, attach the petals to the base of layer 1. Repeat to attach the remaining D petals, making sure that the sets of petals are evenly distributed around layer 1.

11. Stack two E petals together. Curl and cup the petals. Pinch the bottom 2 cm (¾ in) of the petals, then attach them to the base of the flower using parafilm tape. Repeat to attach the remaining E petals, making sure that the pairs of petals are evenly distributed around the previous layer.

Calyx

12. Using olive/moss-green double-sided paper, cut one calyx with template F.

13. Wrap the calyx around the base of the flower so that the sepals are evenly distributed, securing with parafilm tape. Cover the base of the calyx and wrap the rest of the stem with light-green paper strip, securing with PVA glue.

14. Gently curl the sepals outwards.

Leaves

15. Cut three pieces of 22-gauge wire, each 15 cm (6 in) long. Wrap the entire length of each stem with light-green paper strip, securing with PVA glue.

16. Using olive/moss-green double-sided paper and following the Basic Leaf method (page 219, steps 2–8), make three leaves with template G.

17. Adhere the top 3 cm (1¼ in) of each stem to the back of a leaf using PVA glue.

18. Using PVA glue, join the leaf stems together, leaving 1 cm (½ in) between the base of each leaf and the node. Cover the join with light-green paper strip.

Assembly

19. Using PVA glue, attach the bottom 7 cm (2¾ in) of the sprig of leaves to the flower stem, 13 cm (5 in) below the base of the flower. Cover the join with light-green paper strip.

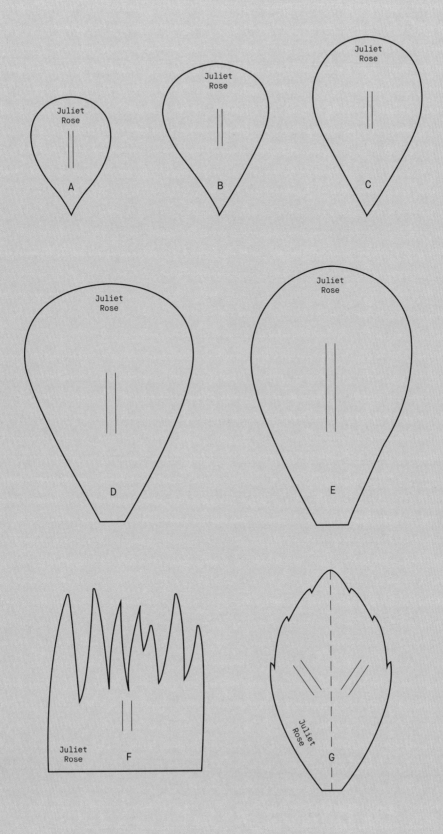

Juliet
Rose

A

Juliet
Rose

B

Juliet
Rose

C

Juliet
Rose

D

Juliet
Rose

E

Juliet
Rose

F

Juliet
Rose

G

Leucadendron

SKILL LEVEL

Beginner

SKILLS REQUIRED

Basics 1–6 (pages 244–245)
Shaping 1–4 (page 246)

NOTE

Dimensions are height x length
Paper grain is vertical

ARRANGEMENT

Frost 4 (page 46)

TOOLS

– Scissors

– Bamboo skewer

– Pliers

– Toothpick

PAPER

– Double-sided crepe paper in red/wine

– Double-sided crepe paper in olive/
  moss green

– 60gsm crepe paper strip in crimson

– 180gsm crepe paper in lime pulp

OTHER MATERIALS

– Flower 14 templates (page 149)

– Glue stick

– 16-gauge wire

– Parafilm tape

– PVA glue

Flowersmith — Flowers

Preparation

1. Using red/wine double-sided paper, cut six petals with template A. Using the glue stick, paste two petals together with the red sides facing each other. Repeat with the remaining petals. Allow to dry, then gently curl all the petals.

2. Using red/wine double-sided paper, cut ten petals with template B. Paste two petals together with the red sides facing each other. Repeat with the remaining petals. Allow to dry, then gently curl all the petals.

3. Using red/wine double-sided paper, cut 24 petals with template C. Paste two petals together with the red sides facing each other. Repeat with the remaining petals. Allow to dry, then gently curl all the petals.

4. Using olive/moss-green double-sided paper, cut 30 leaves with template B. Paste two leaves together with the moss-green sides facing each other. Repeat with the remaining leaves. Allow to dry.

5. Using olive/moss-green double-sided paper, cut 20 leaves with template D. Paste two leaves together with the moss-green sides facing each other. Repeat with the remaining leaves. Allow to dry, then gently curl all the leaves.

Stem

6. Cut three pieces of 16-gauge wire, each 30 cm (12 in) long. Bunch them together and wrap the entire length of the stem with parafilm tape. Wrap the stem with crimson paper strip, securing with PVA glue.

Centre

7. Cut one 2.5 x 20 cm (1 x 8 in) strip of lime-pulp paper. Gently stretch the piece of paper crosswise to increase the width to 30 cm (12 in). Fringe the top 1.5 cm (½ in) of the strip.

8. Wrap the unfringed edge of the paper strip around one end of the stem, gradually moving downwards as you go, so that the fringe covers the top 2–2.5 cm (¾–1 in) of the stem. Secure the end of the fringed paper to the stem using parafilm tape.

9. Trim the fringe into a cone shape.

Petals

10. Layer 1: Using parafilm tape, attach all of the A petals evenly around the base of the flower centre.

11. Layer 2: Attach all of the B petals evenly around the base of layer 1.

12. Layer 3: Attach six C petals evenly around the base of layer 2. Cover the parafilm tape with crimson paper strip.

13. Layer 4: Attach the remaining C petals evenly around the flower centre, 1 cm (½ in) below the base of layer 3. Cover the parafilm tape with crimson paper strip.

Leaves

14. Layer 1: Using parafilm tape, attach seven D leaves evenly around the flower, 1 cm (½ in) below the base of the flower. Cover the tape with crimson paper strip.

15. Layer 2: Attach the remaining D leaves evenly around the flower, 1 cm (½ in) below the base of layer 1. Cover the tape with crimson paper strip.

16. Layer 3: Attach three B leaves evenly around the flower, 3 cm (1¼ in) below the base of layer 2. Cover the tape with crimson paper strip.

17. Layer 4: Attach another three B leaves evenly around the flower, 2 cm (¾ in) below the base of layer 3. Cover the tape with crimson paper strip.

18. Continue to attach the remaining B leaves in the same way. Cover the tape and wrap the remaining stem with crimson paper strip.

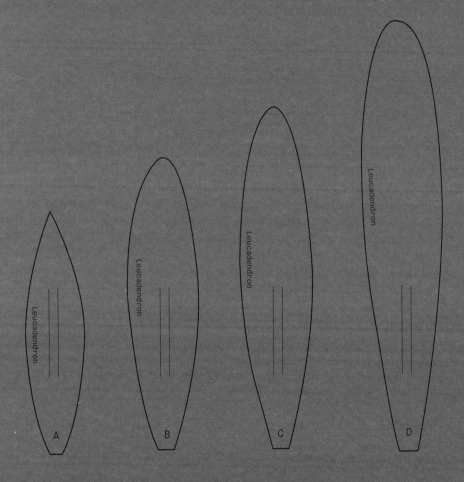

Lily

SKILL LEVEL

Advanced

SKILLS REQUIRED

Basics 1–6 (pages 244–245)
Shaping 1 (page 246)

NOTE

Dimensions are height x length
Paper grain is vertical

ARRANGEMENT

Sunshine 1 (page 16)

TOOLS

- Pliers
- Toothpick
- Scissors
- Bamboo skewer

PAPER

- 60gsm crepe paper strip in yellow
- Double-sided crepe paper in butter/
  yellow
- 60gsm crepe paper strip in light green
- Double-sided crepe paper in olive/
  moss green

OTHER MATERIALS

- 22-gauge wire
- PVA glue
- Flower 15 templates (page 155)
- Paprika
- Parafilm tape

Flowersmith — Flowers

Stamens

1. Cut six pieces of 22-gauge wire, each 40 cm (16 in) long. Wrap the entire length of each wire with yellow paper strip, securing with PVA glue. These will be the filaments (the stalk-like parts) of your stamens.

2. Using butter/yellow double-sided paper, cut six stamen heads with template A. Using PVA glue, adhere one end of a yellow wire to the top half of each stamen head. Bend the wires so each stamen is almost at a right angle to the stem.

3. Use a toothpick to apply PVA glue to the surface of each stamen head, then dip it into paprika. Allow to dry.

4. Using PVA glue, join the six stamen filaments together, leaving 6 cm (2½ in) between the base of each stamen head and the joint. Bend the wires out to open up the stamens. These joined wires will form the main stem.

Petals

5. Cut two pieces of 22-gauge wire, each 45 cm (18 in) long. Wrap the entire length of each wire with yellow paper strip, securing with PVA glue.

6. Cut a 10 x 20 cm (4 x 8 in) piece of butter/yellow double-sided paper. Place the paper on a flat surface with the butter side facing up. Fold down the top left and top right corners to meet on the bottom edge of the paper. Unfold to reveal the creases.

7. Using PVA glue, adhere the wires to the creases. Using a toothpick, apply glue to the paper, then fold the corners in again. Apply pressure to smooth the surface and secure the folds. Allow to dry.

8. Cut down the centre of the paper to separate the triangles.

9. Using PVA glue, join the two triangles along the wired edges so that they are slightly overlapping. Apply pressure to secure the join. Allow to dry.

10. Place the paper square on a flat surface, with the exposed wires closer and perpendicular to your body, making sure that the paper grains are running upwards and outwards from the wires.

11. Place template B on the paper square, so that the spine of the petal aligns with the wire, and the bottom of the template is closest to your body. Cut around the template to make a petal. Gently bend the petal along the wire to make a slight curve.

12. Repeat steps 5–11 to make five more petals.

13. Layer 1: Using PVA glue, attach the exposed wires of three petals to the main flower stem, positioning them evenly around the base of the stamens.

14. Layer 2: Attach the remaining three petals around the base of the flower, between the gaps of the petals in layer 1.

15. Starting from the base of the flower, wrap the length of the stem with light-green paper strip, securing with PVA glue.

$\longrightarrow$

Leaves

16. Using olive/moss-green double-sided paper, cut two leaves with template C. Create a fold down the centre of each leaf to make a spine, then curl gently.

17. Using PVA glue, attach the first leaf to the main stem, 5 cm (2 in) below the base of the flower. Cover the leaf joint with light-green paper strip.

18. Attach the second leaf to the main stem, 5 cm (2 in) below the first leaf. Cover the leaf joint with light-green paper strip.

Buds

19. Cut six pieces of 22-gauge wire, 45 cm (18 in) long. Wrap the entire length of each wire with yellow paper strip, securing with PVA glue.

20. Using template D, make three petals, following steps 6–11 on page 153.

21. Using PVA glue, join the exposed petal wires together. Starting from the base of the petals, wrap the entire length of the stem with light-green paper strip, securing with PVA glue.

22. Gently bend the tips of the petals outwards.

23. Using olive/moss-green double-sided paper, cut three leaves with template C. Create a fold down the centre of each leaf to make a spine.

24. Using PVA glue, attach the first leaf to the stem, 7 cm (2¾ in) below the base of the bud. Cover the leaf joint with light-green paper strip.

25. Attach the second leaf 7 cm (2¾ in) below the first leaf, then cover the leaf joint with light-green paper strip.

26. Attach the third leaf 2 cm (¾ in) below the second leaf, then cover the leaf joint with light-green paper strip.

Assembly

27. Using parafilm tape, join together the bottom 20 cm (8 in) of the bud and flower stems. Cover the tape with light-green paper strip, securing with PVA glue.

Finishing

28. Gently bend the flower and bud stems to create a natural look.

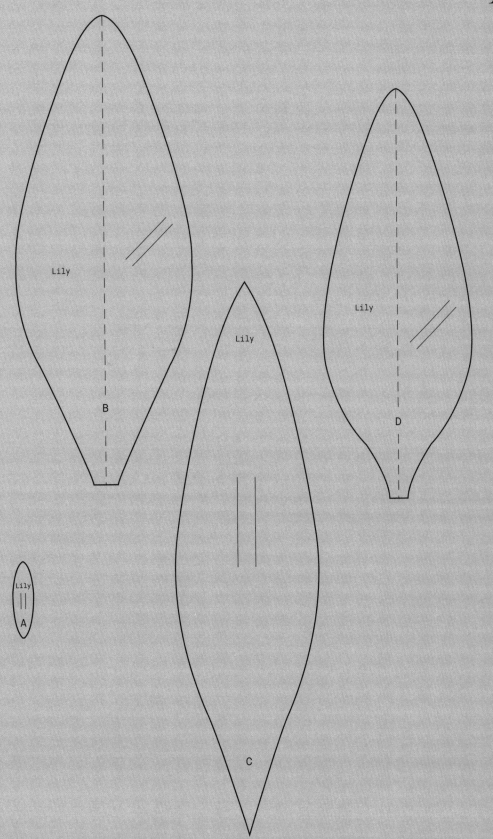

Magnolia Grandiflora

SKILL LEVEL

Beginner

SKILLS REQUIRED

Basics 1-6 (pages 244-245)
Shaping 1, 2, 3 & 5 (page 246)

NOTE

Dimensions are height x length
Paper grain is vertical

ARRANGEMENT

Harvest 2 (page 30)

TOOLS

— Scissors

— Pliers

— Toothpick

— Bamboo skewer

PAPER

— 60gsm crepe paper in white

— 60gsm crepe paper in dark green

— 60gsm crepe paper in light brown

— 60gsm crepe paper strip in dark green

— 180gsm crepe paper in lime pulp

— 60gsm crepe paper in salmon

OTHER MATERIALS

— Glue stick

— 18-gauge wire

— Parafilm tape

— PVA glue

— Flower 16 templates (page 161)

Flowersmith — Flowers

Preparation

1. Cut four 50 x 13 cm (20 x 5 in) pieces of white paper. Using the glue stick, paste all four sheets together. Allow to dry.

2. Cut two 50 x 7 cm (20 x 2¾ in) pieces of dark-green paper. Paste the sheets together, using a minimal amount of glue to avoid discolouration. Allow to dry.

3. Cut two 50 x 7 cm (20 x 2¾ in) pieces of light-brown paper. Paste the sheets together, using a minimal amount of glue. Allow to dry.

4. Paste together the dried dark-green and light-brown sheets. Allow to dry.

Stem

5. Cut three pieces of 18-gauge wire, each 30 cm (12 in) long. Bunch them together and wrap the entire length of the stem with parafilm tape. Wrap the stem with dark-green paper strip, securing with PVA glue.

Centre

6. Cut one 2.5 x 20 cm (1 x 8 in) strip of lime-pulp paper. Gently stretch the strip of paper crosswise to increase the width to 30 cm (12 in). Fringe the top 1.5 cm (½ in) of the strip.

7. Wrap the unfringed edge of the paper strip around one end of the stem, gradually moving downwards as you go, so that the fringe covers the top 2–2.5 cm (¾–1 in) of the stem. Secure with parafilm tape.

8. Trim the fringe into a cone shape.

9. Cut one 2 x 20 cm (¾ x 8 in) strip of salmon paper. Fringe the top 1 cm (½ in) of the strip.

10. Wrap the unfringed edge of the salmon paper strip evenly around the base of the flower centre, securing with parafilm tape.

Petals

11. Using the pasted white paper sheet, cut two petals with template A. Cup the petals. Attach the petals randomly around the base of the flower centre using parafilm tape.

12. Using the pasted white paper sheet, cut seven petals with template B. Use the edge cut-out technique on one or two petals. Cup all of the petals. Attach the petals around the base of the flower centre using parafilm tape.

13. Cover the base of the flower with dark-green paper strip, securing with PVA glue.

Leaves

14. Using the light-brown/dark-green pasted sheet, cut three leaves with template C. With the dark-green side facing up, create a fold down the centre of each leaf to make a spine, then curl gently.

15. Using parafilm tape, attach the first leaf to the stem, 1 cm (½ in) below the base of the flower. Cover the leaf joint with dark-green paper strip.

16. Attach the second leaf to the stem, 1 cm (½ in) below the first leaf. Cover the leaf joint with dark-green paper strip.

17. Attach the third leaf to the stem, 13 cm (5 in) below the second leaf. Cover the leaf joint with dark-green paper strip.

Finishing

18. Gently bend the flower stem to create a natural look.

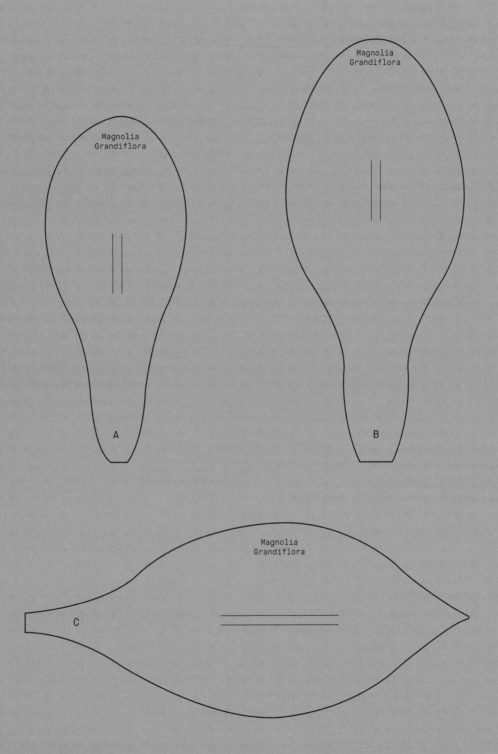

Magnolia
Grandiflora

Magnolia
Grandiflora

A

B

Magnolia
Grandiflora

C

Nasturtium

SKILL LEVEL

Advanced

SKILLS REQUIRED

Basics 1, 4 & 5 (pages 244–245)
Shaping 1, 2 & 4 (page 246)

NOTE

Dimensions are height x length
Paper grain is vertical

ARRANGEMENT

Sunshine 5 (page 24)

TOOLS

- Pliers

- Toothpick

- Scissors

- Bamboo skewer

PAPER

- 60gsm crepe paper strip in light green

- Double-sided crepe paper in orange/
  tangerine

- Double-sided crepe paper in olive/
  moss green

OTHER MATERIALS

- 18-gauge wire

- Parafilm tape

- PVA glue

- 22-gauge wire

- Flower 17 templates (page 167)

- Red marker

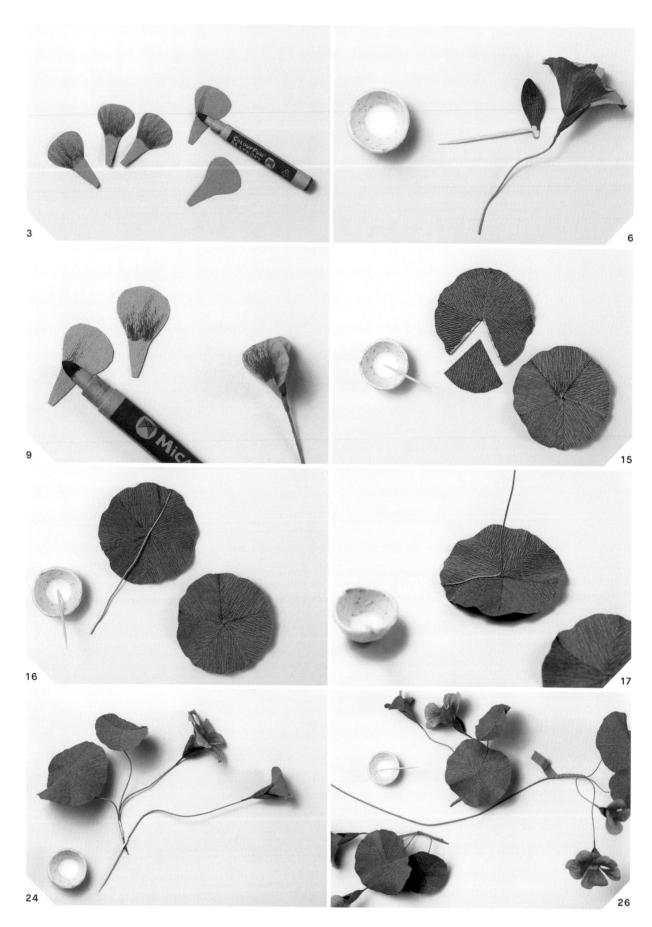

Stem

1. Cut three pieces of 18-gauge wire, each 25 cm (10 in) long. Bunch them together and wrap the entire length of the stem with parafilm tape. Wrap the stem with light-green paper strip, securing with PVA glue.

Large flowers

2. Cut one 11 cm (4¼ in) piece of 22-gauge wire. Wrap the entire length of the stem with light-green paper strip, securing with PVA glue.

3. Using orange/tangerine double-sided paper, cut five petals using template A. With the orange side facing up, brush the edge of the red marker against the petals to colour. Curl each petal outwards, then ruffle the middle of the top edge.

4. Using PVA glue, attach the bottom 1 cm (½ in) of each petal to one end of the stem.

5. Using olive/moss-green double-sided paper, cut two sepals with template B. With the olive side facing up, cup both sepals.

6. Using PVA glue, attach each sepal to the stem, 1–2 cm (½–¾ in) below the base of the flower. Make sure the sepals are opposite each other, with the moss-green sides facing outwards. Cover the base of the sepals with light-green paper strip.

7. Repeat steps 2–6 to make two more large flowers.

Small flowers

8. Cut one 13 cm (5 in) piece of 22-gauge wire. Wrap the entire length of the stem with light-green paper strip, securing with PVA glue.

9. Using orange/tangerine double-sided paper, cut four petals with template C. With the orange side facing up, brush the edge of the red marker against the petals to colour. Curl each petal outwards.

10. Using PVA glue, attach the bottom 1 cm (½ in) of each petal to one end of the stem.

11. Using olive/moss-green double-sided paper, cut two sepals with template B. With the olive side facing up, cup both sepals.

12. Using PVA glue, attach each sepal to the stem, 1–2 cm (½–¾ in) below the base of the flower. Make sure the sepals are opposite each other, with the moss-green sides facing outwards. Cover the base of the sepals with light-green paper strip.

13. Repeat steps 8–12 to make two more small flowers.

Large leaves

14. Cut one 17 cm (6¾ in) piece of 22-gauge wire. Wrap the entire length of the stem with light-green paper strip, securing with PVA glue.

15. Using olive/moss-green double-sided paper, cut five fan shapes with template D. With the olive side facing up, glue the straight edges of all five pieces together using PVA glue, overlapping by a maximum of 3 mm (⅛ in). You will end up with a round leaf. Trim the edge to neaten if necessary.

16. With the olive side still facing up, glue one end of the stems to the leaf: align the stem with one of the joins and attach it from the edge of the leaf to the centre. Allow to dry.

17. Bend the stem at the centre of the leaf to make a right angle.

18. Repeat steps 14–17 to make two more large leaves.

→

Small leaves

19. Cut one 9 cm (3½ in) piece of 22-gauge wire. Wrap the entire length of the stem with light-green paper strip, securing with PVA glue.

20. Using olive/moss-green double-sided paper, cut three fan shapes with template E. With the olive side facing up, glue the straight edges of all three pieces together using PVA glue, overlapping by a maximum of 3 mm (⅛ in). You will end up with a round leaf. Trim the edge to neaten if necessary.

21. With the olive side still facing up, glue one end of the stem to the leaf: align the stem with one of the joins and attach it from the edge of the leaf to the centre. Allow to dry.

22. Bend the stem at the centre of the leaf to make a right angle.

23. Repeat steps 19–22 to make two more small leaves.

Assembly

24. Take one of each flower and each leaf, and use PVA glue to join together the bottom 3 cm (1¼ in) of the stems. Cover the joins with light-green paper strip.

25. Repeat this process to make two more sprigs.

26. Using PVA glue, attach the first sprig firmly to one end of the main stem. Cover the join with light-green paper strip. Attach the remaining two sprigs to the main stem, leaving 8–10 cm (3–4 in) between each sprig. Cover the joins with light-green paper strip.

Finishing

27. Gently bend the stems to create a natural look.

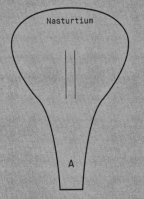

Nasturtium

A

Nasturtium

B

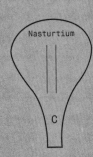

Nasturtium

C

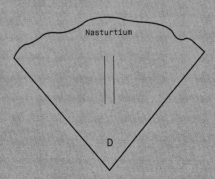

Nasturtium

D

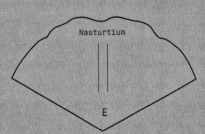

Nasturtium

E

Open Rose

SKILL LEVEL
Intermediate

SKILLS REQUIRED
Basics 1, 4 & 5 (pages 244–245)
Shaping 1, 2, 3 & 5 (page 246)
Colouring 1 & 2 (page 247)

NOTE
Dimensions are height x length
Paper grain is vertical

ARRANGEMENT
Sunshine 4 (page 22)

TOOLS
- Scissors
- Fan paintbrush
- Pliers
- Toothpick
- Bamboo skewer

PAPER
- 60gsm crepe paper in white
- 60gsm crepe paper strip in light green
- 60gsm crepe paper in light brown
- 60gsm crepe paper in yellow
- 60gsm crepe paper in light green

OTHER MATERIALS
- Flower 18 templates (page 173)
- ½ teaspoon yellow food dye
- 2 teaspoons water
- 16-gauge wire
- PVA glue
- Brown marker

Preparation

1. Using white paper, cut five petals with template A and eight petals with template B.

2. Dilute the yellow food dye in the water. Use the dry-wash technique to paint each petal. Allow to dry.

Stem

3. Cut one 22 cm (8¾ in) piece of 16-gauge wire. Wrap the entire length of the stem with light-green paper strip, securing with PVA glue.

Centre

4. Layer 1: Cut one 1.5 x 4 cm (½ x 1½ in) strip of light-brown paper. Fringe the top two-thirds of the strip. Wrap the unfringed edge around one end of the stem and secure with PVA glue.

5. Layer 2: Cut one 2 x 5 cm (¾ x 2 in) strip of yellow paper. Use the brown marker to colour the top 5 mm (¼ in) of the strip. Fringe the top two-thirds, then wrap the unfringed edge around the base of layer 1.

Petals

6. Cup each of the painted petals, then curl the top left and top right edges outwards.

7. Layer 1: Using PVA glue, attach the five A petals evenly around the base of the flower centre, with four cups facing towards the centre and one cup facing away.

8. Layer 2: Attach six of the B petals evenly around the base of layer 1, with five cups facing towards the flower centre and one cup facing away.

9. Layer 3: Attach the remaining two B petals randomly around the base of layer 2, with one cup facing towards the flower centre and one cup facing away.

Calyx

10. Using light-green paper, cut one calyx with template C.

11. Twist and curl the sepals.

12. Wrap the calyx around the base of the flower, so that the sepals are evenly distributed. Secure with PVA glue.

Leaves

13. Using light-green paper, cut four leaves with template D.

14. Cut one 8 cm (3¾ in) piece of 16-gauge wire and one 6 cm (2½ in) piece of wire. Wrap the entire length of each stem with light-green paper strip, securing with PVA glue.

15. Using PVA glue, attach one leaf to the end of the longer stem. Cover the base of the leaf with light-green paper strip. Gently bend the stem.

16. Attach one leaf to the end of the shorter stem. Cover the base of the leaf with light-green paper strip.

17. Attach two more leaves to the shorter stem, on opposite sides of the stem, 1.5 cm (½ in) below the base of the first leaf. Cover the leaf joints with light-green paper strip. Gently bend the stem.

Assembly

18. Using PVA glue, attach the bottom 3 cm (1¼ in) of the single-leaf stem to the main stem, about 9 cm (3½ in) below the base of the flower. Cover the join with light-green paper strip.

19. Attach the bottom 3 cm (1¼ in) of the remaining sprig of leaves to the main stem, about 3 cm (1¼ in) below the leaf joint. Cover the node and wrap the stem with light-green paper strip.

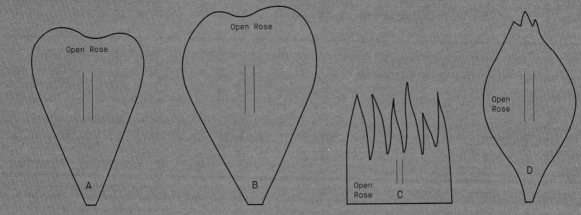

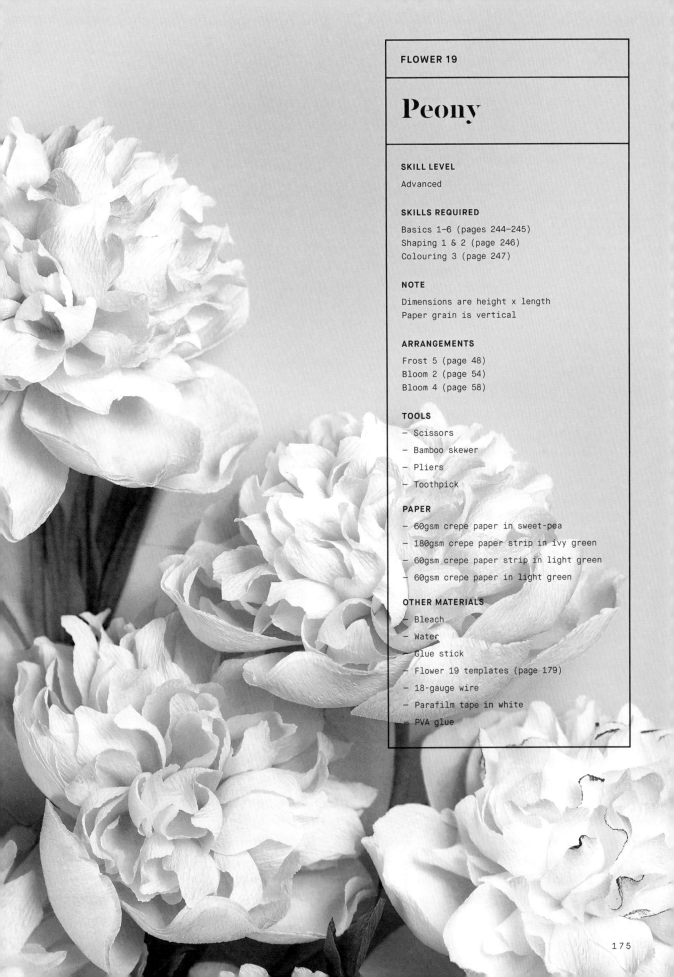

FLOWER 19

Peony

SKILL LEVEL

Advanced

SKILLS REQUIRED

Basics 1–6 (pages 244–245)
Shaping 1 & 2 (page 246)
Colouring 3 (page 247)

NOTE

Dimensions are height x length
Paper grain is vertical

ARRANGEMENTS

Frost 5 (page 48)
Bloom 2 (page 54)
Bloom 4 (page 58)

TOOLS

– Scissors

– Bamboo skewer

– Pliers

– Toothpick

PAPER

– 60gsm crepe paper in sweet-pea

– 180gsm crepe paper strip in ivy green

– 60gsm crepe paper strip in light green

– 60gsm crepe paper in light green

OTHER MATERIALS

– Bleach

– Water

– Glue stick

– Flower 19 templates (page 179)

– 18-gauge wire

– Parafilm tape in white

– PVA glue

Preparation

1. Cut 14 strips of sweet-pea paper, each 7 x 27 cm (2¾ x 10¾ in). Bleach the top 2–3 cm (¾–1¼ in) of the long edge of each strip, one at a time. Allow to dry.

2. Cut three pieces of sweet-pea paper, each 50 x 27 cm (20 x 10¾ in). Paste all three sheets together using the glue stick. Use a minimal amount of glue to avoid discolouration. Allow to dry.

Centre

3. Take one strip of the bleached sweet-pea paper and fold it in half three times. Place template A on top of the paper, aligning the bleached edge with the top of the template. Cut around the template to create eight petals.

4. Stack four petals on top of each other so that they are perfectly aligned. Curl and cup the petals. Repeat with the remaining four petals.

5. Repeat steps 3 and 4 with the remaining paper strips to make 104 more petals.

6. Cut six pieces of 18-gauge wire, each 6 cm (2½ in) long. Wrap the entire length of each stem with parafilm tape.

7. Pinch the bottom 1 cm (½ in) of a petal, then attach the pinched section to the end of a stem using parafilm tape.

8. Attach 11 petals around the base of the first petal using parafilm tape, distributing the petals evenly around the top 1 cm (½ in) of the stem.

9. Repeat this process to make five more florets using the remaining short wires. Gently bend each floret at the base.

10. Cut three pieces of wire, each 25 cm (10 in) long. Bunch them together, then wrap the entire length of the stem with parafilm tape.

11. Using parafilm tape, attach 12 petals to one end of the long stem (as for steps 7–8). Then attach the six florets evenly around the centre, 1.5 cm (½ in) below the base of the petals.

12. Attach the remaining single petals around the the flower centre, so they cover the bases of the florets.

$\longrightarrow$

Petals

13. Using the pasted sweet-pea paper sheet, cut ten petals with template B. Use the edge cut-out technique on two or three petals.

14. Curl and cup the petals, then pinch the bottom 2 cm (¾ in) of each petal.

15. Layer 1: Using parafilm tape, attach five of the petals evenly around the base of the flower centre.

16. Layer 2: Attach the remaining petals evenly around the base of layer 1.

17. Wrap the thin section of the flower stem with ivy-green paper strip to thicken it. Then wrap the entire length of the stem with light-green paper strip, securing with PVA glue.

Leaves

18. Cut two pieces of wire, each 15 cm (6 in) long. Wrap the entire length of each stem with light-green paper strip, securing with PVA glue.

19. Using light-green paper, cut six leaves with template C.

20. Using PVA glue, attach the first leaf to one end of a stem. Cover the base of the leaf with light-green paper strip.

21. Attach two leaves, 2 cm (¾ in) below the base of the first leaf, on opposite sides of the stem. Cover the leaf joints with light-green paper strip. Gently bend the stem.

22. Repeat steps 20 and 21 to make a second sprig of leaves.

Assembly

23. Using parafilm tape, attach the bottom 7 cm (2¾ in) of one sprig of leaves to the flower stem, about 10 cm (4 in) below the base of the flower. Cover the tape with light-green paper strip.

24. Attach the bottom 7 cm (2¾ in) of the remaining sprig of leaves to the flower stem, 2 cm (¾ in) below the first sprig. Cover the tape with light-green paper strip.

Finishing

25. Gently push the large petals down to open up the flower. Bend the flower stem to create a natural look.

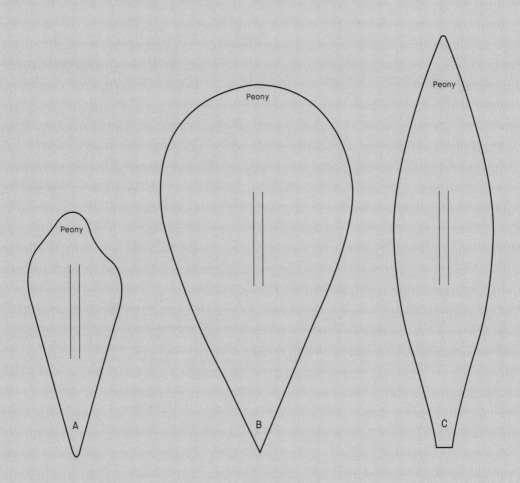

Peony

Peony

Peony

A

B

C

Plum Blossom

SKILL LEVEL

Intermediate

SKILLS REQUIRED

Basics 1–5 (pages 244–245)
Shaping 2 (page 246)

NOTE

Dimensions are height x length
Paper grain is vertical

ARRANGEMENT

Frost 5 (page 48)

TOOLS

– Scissors
– Pliers
– Toothpick
– Bamboo skewer

PAPER

– 60gsm crepe paper in white
– 60gsm crepe paper in dark brown
– 60gsm crepe paper strip in dark brown
– 60gsm crepe paper in hydrangea

OTHER MATERIALS

– PVA glue
– Ground turmeric
– Flower 20 templates (page 185)
– 18-gauge wire
– Parafilm tape
– 22-gauge wire
– Cotton wool

Preparation

1. Using white paper, cut 21 rectangles, each 2.5 x 2 cm (1 x ¾ in). Fringe the top 2 cm (¾ in) of each piece. Lightly dip the tips of the fringe into PVA glue, then into ground turmeric. Shake off any excess turmeric, then allow to dry.

2. Using dark-brown paper, cut 93 sepals with template A.

Branch & stems

3. Cut three pieces of 18-gauge wire, each 40 cm (16 in) long. Bunch them together and wrap the entire length of the wire with parafilm tape. Wrap the stem with dark-brown paper strip, securing with PVA glue. This will be the main branch.

4. Cut 31 pieces of 22-gauge wire, each 5 cm (2 in) long. Wrap the entire length of each wire with dark-brown paper strip, securing with PVA glue. These will be the stems of the buds and flowers.

Buds

5. Cut ten 4 x 4 cm (1½ x 1½ in) squares of hydrangea paper.

6. Put a small amount of cotton wool around one end of a short stem to form a ball. Cover the cotton wool ball with a hydrangea paper square. Use parafilm tape to secure the paper to the stem, then cover the tape with dark-brown paper strip. Use PVA glue to attach three sepals evenly around the base of the bud.

7. Glue the tips of the sepals to the bud.

8. Repeat steps 6 and 7 to make nine more buds. For a natural look, make them in slightly different sizes, trimming the paper squares if required.

Flowers

9. Using hydrangea paper, cut 105 petals with template B. Cup all the petals. (To hasten this process, stack several pieces of paper together before cutting and cupping, making sure that the grains are aligned.)

10. Take a fringed piece of white paper and wrap the unfringed edge around one end of a short stem, securing with PVA glue.

11. Attach five petals around the base of the fringed centre.

12. Attach three sepals around the base of the flower.

13. Cover the base of the flower with dark-brown paper strip.

14. About 2 cm (¾ in) below the base of the flower, gently bend the stem.

15. Repeat steps 10–14 to make 20 more flowers.

16. Take three flowers and join the bottom 2.5 cm (1 in) of the stems together using PVA glue. Cover the join with dark-brown paper strip. Repeat this process to make six more flower triplets.

Assembly

17. Using PVA glue, attach the bottom 4 cm (1½ in) of one bud stem to the main branch, 2 cm (¾ in) from the top end. Continue attaching buds and flower triplets along the branch, working in a downwards spiral. Most of the buds should be positioned along the top section of the branch, either by themselves or among the flowers. Cover the nodes with dark-brown paper strip as you go.

Finishing

18. To stabilise the branch, add additional wire below the last flower triplet, then wrap with dark-brown paper strip.

NOTE

To make a large branch, make several of these branches and join them together. Change the quantity of the buds and flowers on each branch for a natural look.

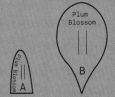

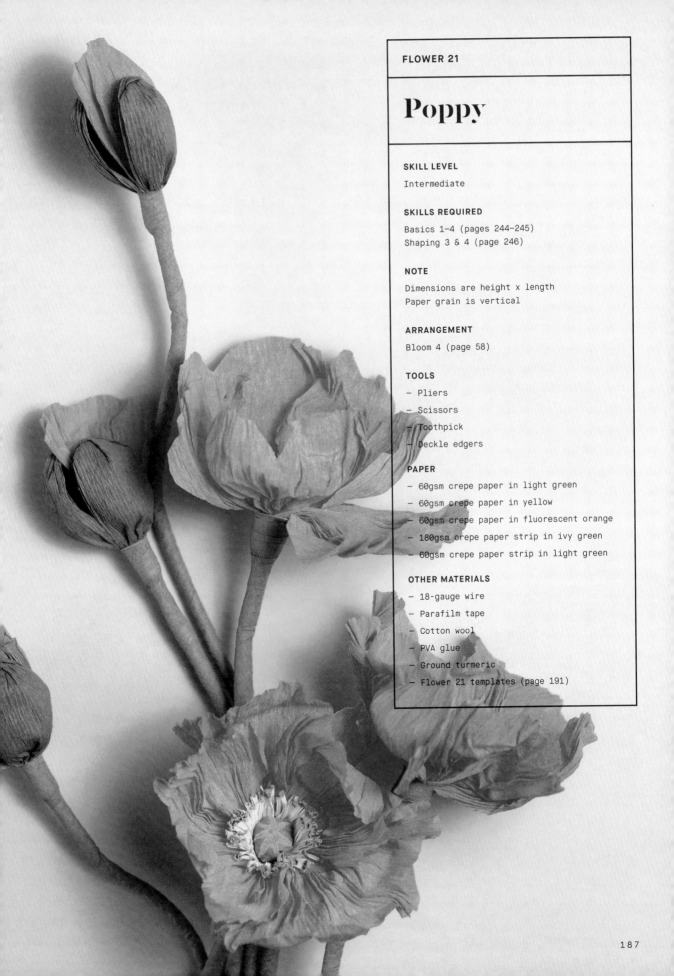

Poppy

SKILL LEVEL

Intermediate

SKILLS REQUIRED

Basics 1–4 (pages 244–245)
Shaping 3 & 4 (page 246)

NOTE

Dimensions are height x length
Paper grain is vertical

ARRANGEMENT

Bloom 4 (page 58)

TOOLS

- Pliers
- Scissors
- Toothpick
- Deckle edgers

PAPER

- 60gsm crepe paper in light green
- 60gsm crepe paper in yellow
- 60gsm crepe paper in fluorescent orange
- 180gsm crepe paper strip in ivy green
- 60gsm crepe paper strip in light green

OTHER MATERIALS

- 18-gauge wire
- Parafilm tape
- Cotton wool
- PVA glue
- Ground turmeric
- Flower 21 templates (page 191)

Stem

1. Cut three pieces of 18-gauge wire, each 30 cm (12 in) long. Bunch them together and wrap the entire length of the stem with parafilm tape.

Centre

2. Cut one 5 x 5 cm (2 x 2 in) square of light-green paper.

3. Put a small amount of cotton wool around one end of the stem to form a ball. Cover the cotton wool ball with the light-green paper square. Use parafilm tape to secure the paper to the stem.

4. Use a toothpick to apply PVA glue to the centre of the flower in the shape of a flower pistil. Gently dip the flower centre into ground turmeric, lightly tapping off any excess. Allow to dry completely.

Stamens

5. Cut one 3 x 20 cm (1¼ x 8 in) strip of yellow paper. Gently stretch the piece of paper crosswise to increase the width to approximately 30 cm (12 in). Finely fringe the top 2 cm (¾ in) of the strip.

6. Fold the fringed paper in half five times, until it resembles a tassel. Gently twist the fringe back and forth several times, then unwrap the paper strip completely.

7. Wrap the unfringed edge of the strip around the base of the flower centre, securing with PVA glue.

8. Holding the stem, lightly dip the tips of the fringe into PVA glue, then into ground turmeric. Shake off any excess turmeric, then allow to dry.

Petals

9. Using fluorescent-orange paper, cut four petals with template A. Trim the top edge of each petal with deckle edgers.

10. Scrunch each petal into a small ball, then open without stretching the paper.

11. Layer 1: Gather and pinch the bottom 1 cm (½ in) of a petal, then attach it to the base of the flower centre with parafilm tape. Attach a second petal opposite the first petal.

12. Layer 2: Attach the remaining two petals opposite each other, below layer 1.

13. Starting from the base of the flower, wrap the entire length of the stem with ivy-green paper strip to thicken it, securing with PVA glue. Repeat once.

14. Wrap the entire length of the stem with light-green paper strip, securing with PVA glue.

15. Gently bend the stem to form an 'S' shape.

Bud

16. Cut three pieces of wire, each 30 cm (12 in) long. Bunch them together and wrap the entire length of the stem with parafilm tape.

17. Cut four 11 x 3 cm (4¼ x 1¼ in) pieces of light-green paper. Stack two of the pieces on top of each other. Twist once in the centre, then fold in half to create a twisted sepal. Repeat with the remaining pieces of paper to make another sepal. Cup both sepals.

18. Take one sepal and pinch the bottom 1 cm (½ in), then attach the pinched end to the end of the stem using parafilm tape.

19. Using fluorescent-orange paper, cut one petal with template B. Gather and pinch the bottom 1 cm (½ in) of the petal, then attach it to the end of the stem.

20. Attach the second sepal opposite the first, adjusting the petal so that it protrudes from the bud.

21. Starting from the base of the bud, wrap the entire length of the stem with ivy-green paper strip to thicken it, securing with PVA glue. Repeat once.

22. Wrap the entire length of the stem with light-green paper strip, securing with PVA glue.

23. Gently bend the stem to form an S shape.

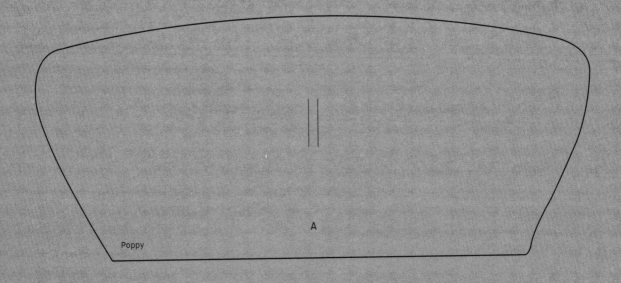

A

Poppy

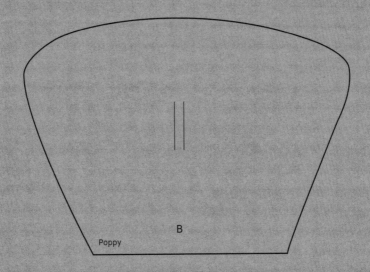

B

Poppy

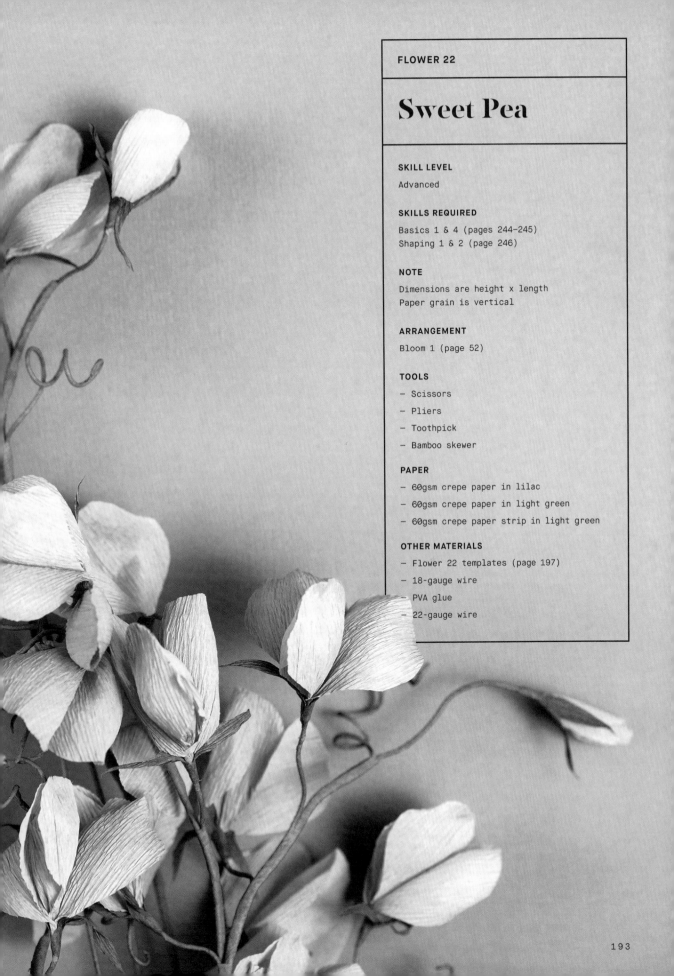

Sweet Pea

SKILL LEVEL
Advanced

SKILLS REQUIRED
Basics 1 & 4 (pages 244–245)
Shaping 1 & 2 (page 246)

NOTE
Dimensions are height x length
Paper grain is vertical

ARRANGEMENT
Bloom 1 (page 52)

TOOLS

– Scissors

– Pliers

– Toothpick

– Bamboo skewer

PAPER

– 60gsm crepe paper in lilac

– 60gsm crepe paper in light green

– 60gsm crepe paper strip in light green

OTHER MATERIALS

– Flower 22 templates (page 197)

– 18-gauge wire

– PVA glue

– 22-gauge wire

Preparation

1. Using lilac paper, cut ten petals with template A, three petals with template B and six petals with template C. Separate the petals by template. Cup all of the B and C petals.

2. Using light-green paper, cut four calyxes with template D.

Stems

3. Cut one 30 cm (12 in) piece of 18-gauge wire. Wrap the entire length of the wire with light-green paper strip, securing with PVA glue. This will be the main stem.

4. Cut four pieces of 22-gauge wire, each 7 cm (2¾ in) long. Wrap the entire length of each wire with light-green paper strip, securing with PVA glue. These will be the stems of the bud and flowers.

Tendril

5. Cut one 10 cm (4 in) piece of 22-gauge wire. Wrap the entire length of the wire with light-green paper strip, securing with PVA glue.

6. Wind the top 7 cm (2¾ in) of the wire around a small pencil. Remove the tendril from the pencil, then gently stretch the curl.

Bud

7. Using PVA glue, attach the bottom 1 cm (½ in) of four A petals evenly around one end of a short stem.

8. Take one calyx and twist the tips of the sepals. Using PVA glue, attach the bottom 1 cm (½ in) of the calyx around the base of the bud.

9. Curl the sepals outwards. Cover the base of the calyx with light-green paper strip.

Flowers

10. Layer 1: Using PVA glue, attach the bottom 1 cm (½ in) of two A petals to one end of a short stem.

11. Layer 2: Fold one B petal in half along its spine, cup each side, then glue the bottom 5 mm (¼ in) of the petal to the base of layer 1. Glue the tips together to close the B petal.

12. Layer 3: Attach the bottom 5 mm (¼ in) of two C petals to the base of layer 2, one on each side of the B petal and overlapping each other by 3 mm (⅛ in). Glue the overlapping edges together. Curl the top of the C petals outwards.

13. Take one calyx and twist the tips of the sepals. Attach the bottom 1 cm (½ in) of the calyx to the base of the flower using PVA glue. Curl the sepals outwards, then cover the base of the calyx with light-green paper strip.

14. Repeat steps 10–13 to make two more flowers.

Assembly

15. Using PVA glue, join the bottom 3 cm (1¼ in) of the bud stem to the top end of the main stem. Cover the join with light-green paper strip.

16. Attach the bottom 3 cm (1¼ in) of one flower stem to the main stem, 7 cm (2¾ in) below the base of the bud. Cover the join with light-green paper strip.

17. Attach a second flower to the main stem, 3 cm (1¼ in) below the node of the first flower stem. Cover the join with light-green paper strip.

18. Attach the third flower to the main stem, about 4 cm (1½ in) below the node of the second flower stem. Cover the join with light-green paper strip.

19. Attach the tendril to the main stem, about 4 cm (1½ in) below the lowest node. Cover the join with light-green paper strip.

Finishing

20. Gently bend all the stems to create a natural look.

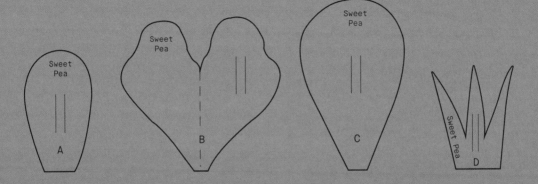

Zinnia

SKILL LEVEL

Beginner

SKILLS REQUIRED

Basics 1, 4 & 5 (pages 244–245)
Shaping 1 & 3 (page 246)

NOTE

Dimensions are height x length
Paper grain is vertical

ARRANGEMENT

Harvest 1 (page 28)

TOOLS

- Pliers
- Toothpick
- Scissors
- Bamboo skewer

PAPER

- 60gsm crepe paper strip in light green
- 60gsm crepe paper in light brown
- 60gsm crepe paper in yellow
- Double-sided crepe paper in lavender/ orchid
- Double-sided crepe paper in olive/ moss green

OTHER MATERIALS

- 18-gauge wire
- Parafilm tape
- PVA glue
- Flower 23 templates (page 203)

Stem

1. Cut three pieces of 18-gauge wire, each 25 cm (10 in) long. Bunch them together and wrap the entire length of the stem with parafilm tape. Wrap the stem with light-green paper strip, securing with PVA glue.

Centre

2. Cut one 1 x 10 cm (½ x 4 in) strip of light-brown paper, one 2 x 12 cm (¾ x 4¾ in) strip of light-brown paper, and one 2 x 12 cm (¾ x 4¾ in) strip of yellow paper. Fringe the top two-thirds of each paper strip.

3. Layer 1: Wrap the unfringed edge of the shorter light-brown strip around one end of the stem, securing with PVA glue.

4. Layer 2: Wrap the yellow strip around the base of layer 1, securing with PVA glue.

5. Layer 3: Wrap the second light-brown strip around the base of layer 2, securing with PVA glue.

Petals

6. Using lavender/orchid double-sided paper, cut eight petals with template A and 48 petals with template B. (To hasten this process, stack several pieces of paper together before cutting, making sure that the grains are aligned.) Curl all the petals.

7. Layer 1: Using PVA glue, attach all of the A petals evenly around the base of the flower centre.

8. Layer 2: Attach 12 of the B petals evenly around the base of layer 1.

9. Layers 3–5: Attach 12 of the B petals evenly around the base of the previous layer.

10. Cover the base of the flower with light-green paper strip, securing with PVA glue.

Leaves

11. Using the olive/moss-green double-sided paper and following the Basic Leaf method (page 219, steps 2–8), make two leaves with template C.

12. Use PVA glue to attach the leaves to opposite sides of the stem, 10 cm (4 in) below the base of the flower.

Finishing

13. Bend the stem and curl the leaves to create a natural look.

NOTE

You can also use direct leaf cutting method 2 (page 219) to make the leaves.

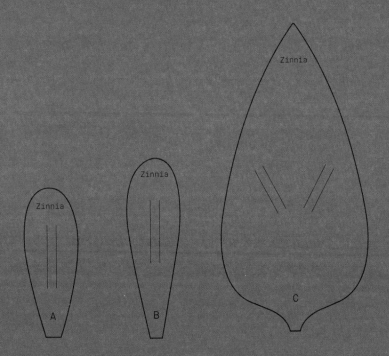

Foliage

Air Plant

SKILL LEVEL
Beginner

SKILLS REQUIRED
Basics 1, 2, 3 & 5 (page 244–245)
Shaping 1 (page 246)

NOTE
Dimensions are height x length
Paper grain is vertical

ARRANGEMENT
Frost 3 (page 44)

TOOLS
– Pliers
– Scissors
– Bamboo skewer
– Toothpick

PAPER
– Double-sided crepe paper in olive/
  moss green
– 60gsm crepe paper strip in light green

OTHER MATERIALS
– 18-gauge wire
– Parafilm tape in white
– Foliage 1 templates (page 209)
– PVA glue

4

5

9

11

Stem

1. Cut three pieces of 18-gauge wire, each 20 cm (8 in) long. Bunch them together, then wrap the entire length of the stem with parafilm tape.

Leaves

2. Using olive/moss-green double-sided paper, cut eight leaves with template A, eight leaves with template B, ten leaves with template C, ten leaves with template D, 12 leaves with template E and 12 leaves with template F. (To hasten this process, stack several pieces of paper together before cutting, making sure that the grains are aligned.) Separate the leaves by template.

3. Hold the bottom of one leaf with your thumb and index finger, with the olive side facing up. Gently curl the top half of the leaf outwards. Repeat to curl all the leaves.

4. Layer 1: Using parafilm tape, attach the bottom 2 cm (¾ in) of all the A leaves evenly around one end of the stem, making sure that the leaves curl outwards from the centre.

5. Layer 2: Attach the bottom 2 cm (¾ in) of all the B leaves to the stem, 5 mm (¼ in) below the first layer, arranging them between the gaps of the leaves in layer 1.

6. Layer 3: Attach the bottom 3 cm (1¼ in) of all the C leaves to the stem, 5 mm (¼ in) below the second layer, arranging them between the gaps of the leaves in layer 2.

7. Layer 4: Attach the bottom 3 cm (1¼ in) of all the D leaves to the stem, 5 mm (¼ in) below layer 3.

8. Layer 5: Attach the bottom 4 cm (1½ in) of all E leaves to the stem, 5 mm (¼ in) below layer 4.

9. Layer 6: Attach the bottom 4 cm (1½ in) of all F leaves to the stem, 5 mm (¼ in) below layer 5.

10. Cover the base of the last layer and wrap the length of the stem with light-green paper strip. Secure with PVA glue.

Finishing

11. To make a stand-alone Air Plant, bend the bottom of the stem to create a stand.

A   B   C   D   E   F

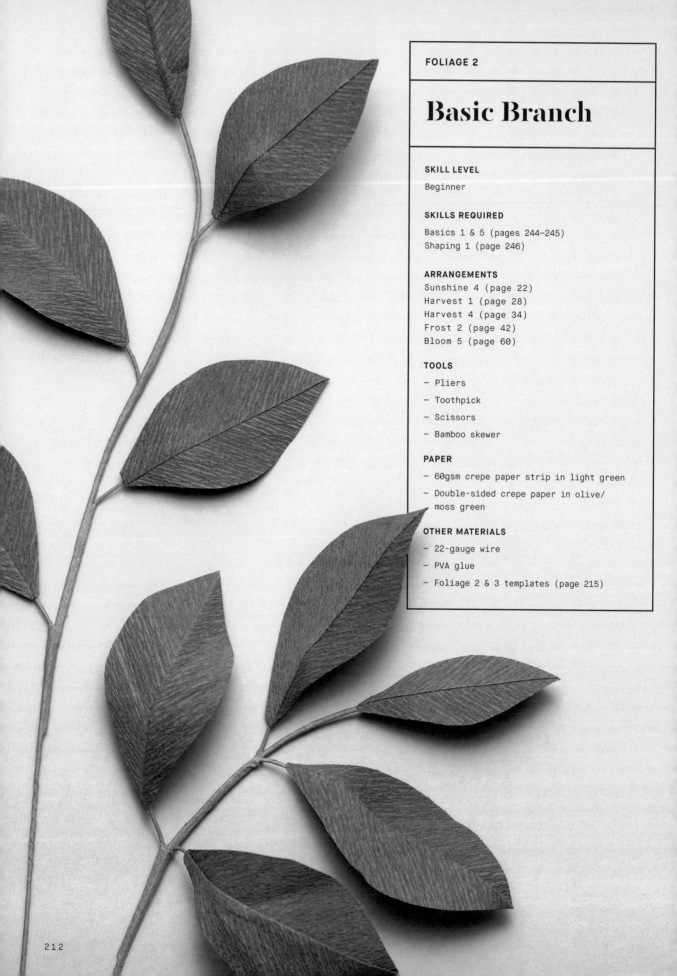

Basic Branch

SKILL LEVEL

Beginner

SKILLS REQUIRED

Basics 1 & 5 (pages 244–245)
Shaping 1 (page 246)

ARRANGEMENTS

Sunshine 4 (page 22)
Harvest 1 (page 28)
Harvest 4 (page 34)
Frost 2 (page 42)
Bloom 5 (page 60)

TOOLS

– Pliers

– Toothpick

– Scissors

– Bamboo skewer

PAPER

– 60gsm crepe paper strip in light green

– Double-sided crepe paper in olive/
  moss green

OTHER MATERIALS

– 22-gauge wire

– PVA glue

– Foliage 2 & 3 templates (page 215)

4

A

B

Preparation

1. Cut one 25 cm (10 in) piece of 22-gauge wire. Wrap the entire length of the wire with light-green paper strip, securing with PVA glue. This will be the main branch.

2. Cut four pieces of wire, each 9 cm (3½ in) long. Wrap the entire length of each wire with light-green paper strip, securing with PVA glue. These will be the leaf stems.

3. Using the double-sided olive/moss-green paper and following the Basic Leaf method (page 219, steps 2–8), make one leaf with template A, two leaves with template B and two leaves with template C.

4. Using PVA glue, attach leaf A to one end of the main branch. Attach each of the remaining leaves to a short stem.

Continue with either the alternating leaf arrangement (see photo A) or the opposite leaf arrangement (see photo B).

Leaf arrangement

A. ALTERNATING LEAF ARRANGEMENT

5. Using PVA glue, attach the bottom 5 cm (2 in) of one B leaf stem to the main branch, 5 cm (2 in) below the base of the A leaf. Allow to dry, then cover the join with light-green paper strip.

6. Attach the second B leaf stem to the opposite side of the main branch, 5 cm (2 in) below the node. Cover the join with light-green paper strip.

7. Repeat steps 1–2 to attach the two C leaves to the main branch.

8. Curl all the leaves. Gently bend the branch to create a natural look.

B. OPPOSITE LEAF ARRANGEMENT

5. Using PVA glue, join together the bottom 5 cm (2 in) of the two B leaf stems.

6. Attach the B leaf sprig to the main branch, 5 cm (2 in) below the base of the A leaf. Cover the join with light-green paper strip.

7. Using PVA glue, join together the bottom 5 cm (2 in) of the two C leaf stems.

8. Attach the C leaf sprig to the main branch, 5 cm (2 in) below the node. Cover the join with light-green paper strip.

9. Curl all the leaves. Gently bend the branch to create a natural look.

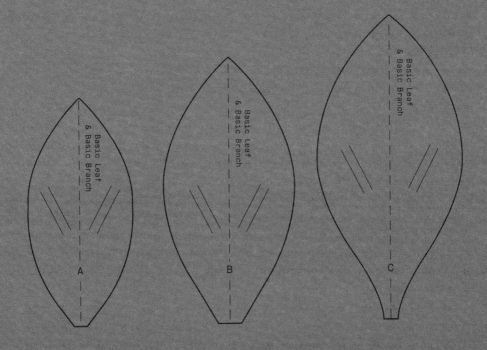

Basic Leaf
& Basic Branch

A

Basic Leaf
& Basic Branch

B

Basic Leaf
& Basic Branch

C

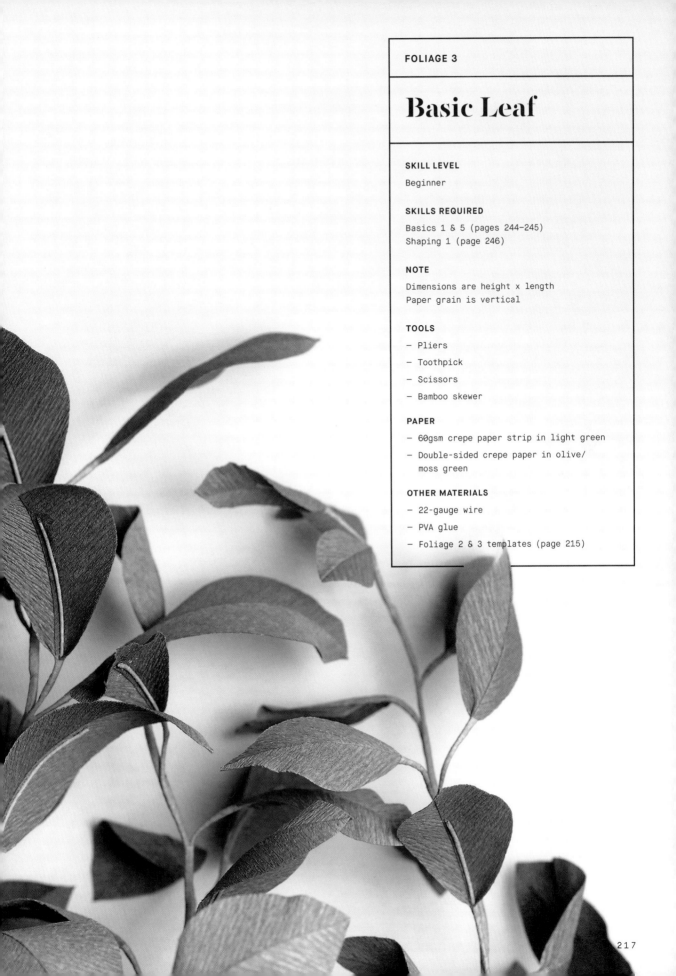

Basic Leaf

SKILL LEVEL

Beginner

SKILLS REQUIRED

Basics 1 & 5 (pages 244–245)
Shaping 1 (page 246)

NOTE

Dimensions are height x length
Paper grain is vertical

TOOLS

– Pliers
– Toothpick
– Scissors
– Bamboo skewer

PAPER

– 60gsm crepe paper strip in light green
– Double-sided crepe paper in olive/
  moss green

OTHER MATERIALS

– 22-gauge wire
– PVA glue
– Foliage 2 & 3 templates (page 215)

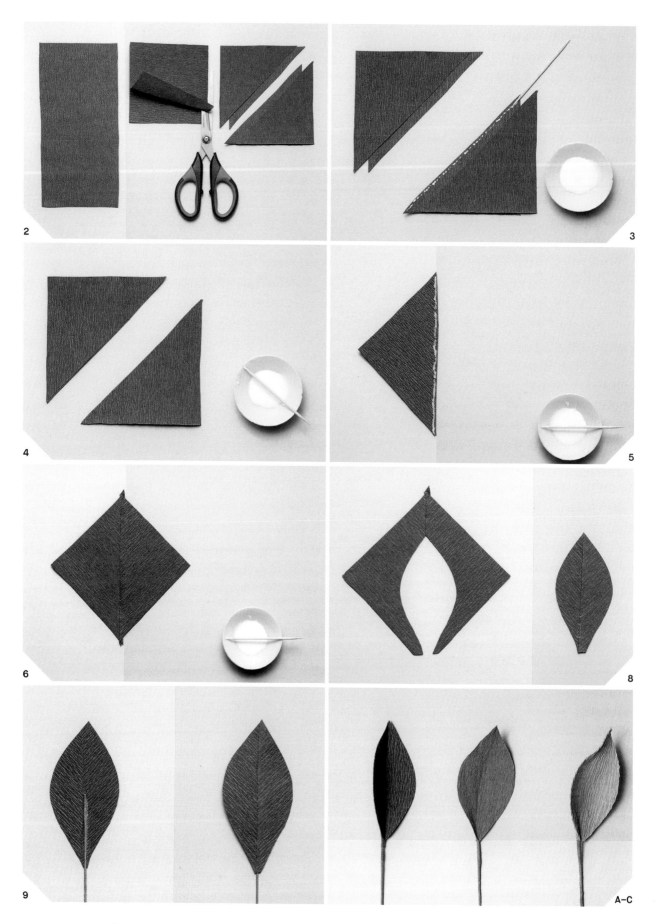

Stem

1. Cut one 9 cm (3½ in) piece of 22-gauge wire. Wrap the entire length of the stem with light-green paper strip, securing with PVA glue.

Leaf

2. Cut one 16 x 8 cm (6¼ x 3¼ in) piece of olive/moss-green double-sided paper, then place it on a flat surface with the desired colour facing up. Fold the paper in half across the grain, then cut along the fold to create two squares. Holding firmly, cut the squares across the diagonal to make two pairs of triangles. Keep each triangle pair together.

3. Place one triangle pair on a flat surface. Slide the top triangle across about 5 mm (¼ in), to reveal the hypotenuse (long side) of the bottom triangle. Use a toothpick to apply a small amount of PVA glue along the hypotenuse of the bottom triangle.

4. Slide the top triangle back into place, gluing the two hypotenuses together. Gently press down with your thumb to secure the join. Allow the glue to dry completely.

5. Once the glue has dried, use a toothpick to apply a small amount of PVA glue along the hypotenuse of the top triangle.

6. Holding the bottom triangle with one hand, use your other hand to open the top triangle as far as you can. Use your thumb to gently press down on the fold, securing the join. Allow to dry completely.

7. Place the paper on your work surface with the fold (spine) perpendicular to your body, and with the paper grains running upwards and outwards from the spine.

8. Place the template (see Note) on top of the piece of paper, with the spines aligned and the bottom of the template closest to your body. Cut around the template to make a leaf.

Assembly

9. Adhere the top 3 cm (1¼ in) of the stem to the back of the leaf using PVA glue.

10. Gently curl the top part of the leaf.

Alternative methods

This project can be time consuming when you are making large flower arrangements. The following direct leaf cutting methods may be used for faster results.

A. Direct leaf cutting using 180gsm paper:
    Cut one or more leaves from the paper using the template (see Note). Curl and cup each leaf, then attach to a stem using PVA glue or parafilm tape.

B. Direct leaf cutting using 60gsm paper:
    Cut one or more leaves from the paper using the template (see Note), then create a fold along the spine of each leaf. Curl each leaf, then attach to a stem using PVA glue or parafilm tape.

C. Direct leaf cutting using double-sided paper:
    Cut one or more leaves from the paper using the template (see Note), then create a fold along the spine of each leaf. Attach each leaf to a stem using PVA glue or parafilm tape.

> **NOTE**
>
> If you are making a Basic Leaf, use template A on page 215. If you are using the Basic Leaf method for another project, use the template referenced in that project.

Basic Vine

SKILL LEVEL

Beginner

SKILLS REQUIRED

Basics 1 & 5 (page 244–245)
Shaping 1 (page 246)

ARRANGEMENT

Harvest 1 (page 28)

TOOLS

- Pliers

- Toothpick

- Scissors

- Bamboo skewer

PAPER

- Double-sided crepe paper in olive/
  moss-green

- 60gsm crepe paper strip in light green

OTHER MATERIALS

- 22-gauge wire

- PVA glue

2

3

Branches

1. Using olive/moss-green double-sided paper, make multiple Basic Branches (page 212).

Assembly

2. Using PVA glue, join together the bottom 5–7 cm (2–2¾ in) of two branches. Cover the join with light-green paper strip.

3. Add extra wire to the bottom of the vine. Cover with light-green paper strip, securing with PVA glue.

4. Continue adding more branches, one at a time. Add extra wire to the stem as you go, to extend and strengthen the vine.

Eucalyptus Branch

SKILL LEVEL

Beginner

SKILLS REQUIRED

Basics 1 & 5 (pages 244–245)

NOTE

Dimensions are height x length
Paper grain is horizontal

ARRANGEMENTS

Frost 3 (page 44)
Frost 4 (page 46)
Bloom 2 (page 54)

TOOLS

− Pliers

− Toothpick

− Scissors

PAPER

− 60gsm crepe paper strip in light green

− 60gsm crepe paper in light green

OTHER MATERIALS

− 18-gauge wire

− PVA glue

− 22-gauge wire

− Foliage 5 template (page 227)

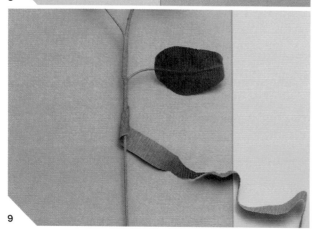

Branch & stems

1. Cut one 43 cm (17 in) piece of 18-gauge wire. Wrap the entire length of the wire with light-green paper strip, securing with PVA glue. This will be the main branch.

2. Cut eight pieces of 22-gauge wire, each 7 cm (2¾ in) long. Wrap the entire length of each wire with light-green paper strip, securing with PVA glue. These will be the leaf stems.

Leaves

3. Using light-green paper, cut 18 leaves with template A.

4. Put one leaf on a flat surface, with the bottom end closest to your body. Using a toothpick, dab a small amount of PVA glue down the centre spine of the leaf.

5. Place one end of the long piece of wire onto the spine of the leaf and gently press down with your thumb to secure the wire to the paper.

6. Dab PVA glue around the edge of the leaf and on the wire, using a minimal amount of glue to avoid discolouration.

7. Take a second leaf and place it on top of the first leaf, making sure they align perfectly. Press down gently to secure the join.

8. Repeat steps 3–7 with the remaining leaves and short wires, to make eight more finished leaves. Slightly bend the stem of each leaf. Allow to dry.

Assembly

9. Using PVA glue, attach the bottom 2.5 cm (1 in) of each of the leaf stems to the main branch. The leaves should be in an alternating arrangement (see page 213), with 2–4 cm (¾–1½ in) between the nodes. Cover the joins with light-green paper strip.

Finishing

10. Gently bend the branch to create a natural look.

NOTE

To make a bigger branch, join multiple branches together.

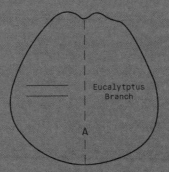

Eucalytptus
Branch

A

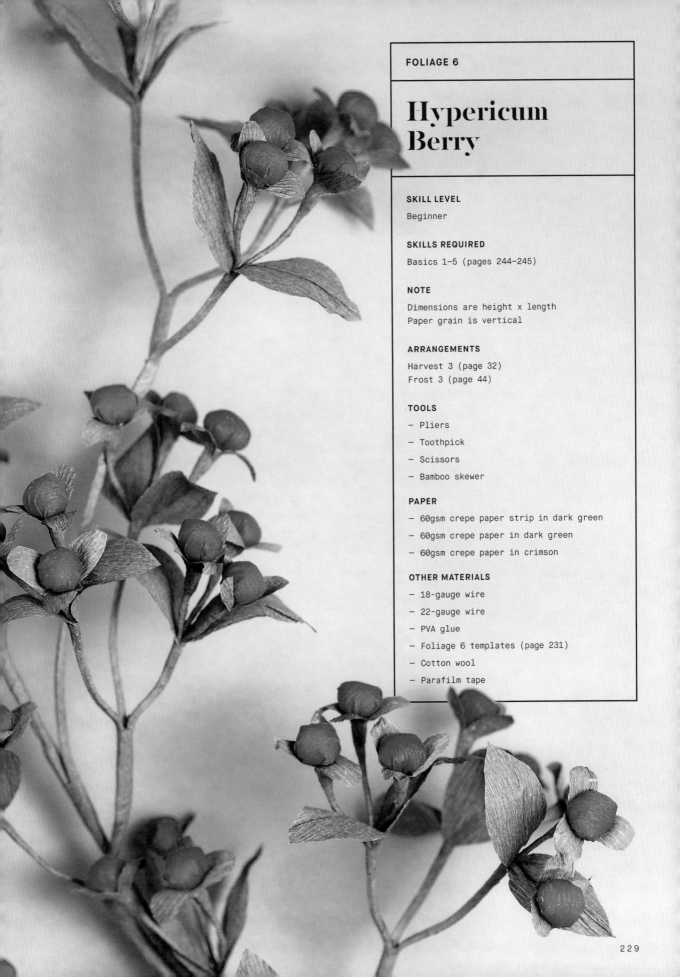

Hypericum Berry

SKILL LEVEL

Beginner

SKILLS REQUIRED

Basics 1–5 (pages 244–245)

NOTE

Dimensions are height x length
Paper grain is vertical

ARRANGEMENTS

Harvest 3 (page 32)
Frost 3 (page 44)

TOOLS

– Pliers
– Toothpick
– Scissors
– Bamboo skewer

PAPER

– 60gsm crepe paper strip in dark green
– 60gsm crepe paper in dark green
– 60gsm crepe paper in crimson

OTHER MATERIALS

– 18-gauge wire
– 22-gauge wire
– PVA glue
– Foliage 6 templates (page 231)
– Cotton wool
– Parafilm tape

5

8

9

12

Berry sprigs

1. Cut one 25 cm (10 in) piece of 18-gauge wire. Then cut two pieces of 22-gauge wire, each 12 cm (4¾ in) long. Wrap the entire length of each stem with dark-green paper strip, securing with PVA glue.

2. Using dark-green paper, cut three calyxes using template A.

3. Cut three 4 x 4 cm (1½ x 1½ in) squares of crimson paper.

4. Put a small amount of cotton wool around one end of the long stem to form a ball. Cover the cotton ball with a crimson paper square. Use parafilm tape to secure the paper to the stem, then cover the tape with dark-green paper strip.

5. Wrap one calyx around the base of the berry, so that the sepals are evenly distributed. Secure with PVA glue. Cover the base of the calyx with dark-green paper strip. Gently curl the sepals outwards.

6. Repeat steps 4 and 5, using the shorter stems and remaining calyxes and crimson squares, to make two more berries.

7. Using dark-green paper and following the Basic Leaf method (page 219, steps 2–8), make two leaves with template B.

8. Using PVA glue, join the three berry stems together, leaving 5 cm (2 in) between the base of the berries and the node. Cover the join with dark-green paper strip.

9. Using PVA glue, attach the two leaves to the main stem at the node, on opposite sides of the stem. Cover the leaf joints with dark-green paper strip.

10. Repeat steps 1–9 to make two more sprigs of berries.

Leaves

11. Using dark-green paper, make two leaves with template B.aa

Assembly

12. Using PVA glue, join the stems of the three berry sprigs together, 5 cm (2 in) below the nodes. Cover the joins with dark-green paper strip.

13. Using PVA glue, attach the leaves to the main stem at the lower node, on opposite sides of the stem. Cover the leaf joints with dark-green paper strip.

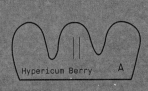

Hypericum Berry   A

Hypericum Berry

B

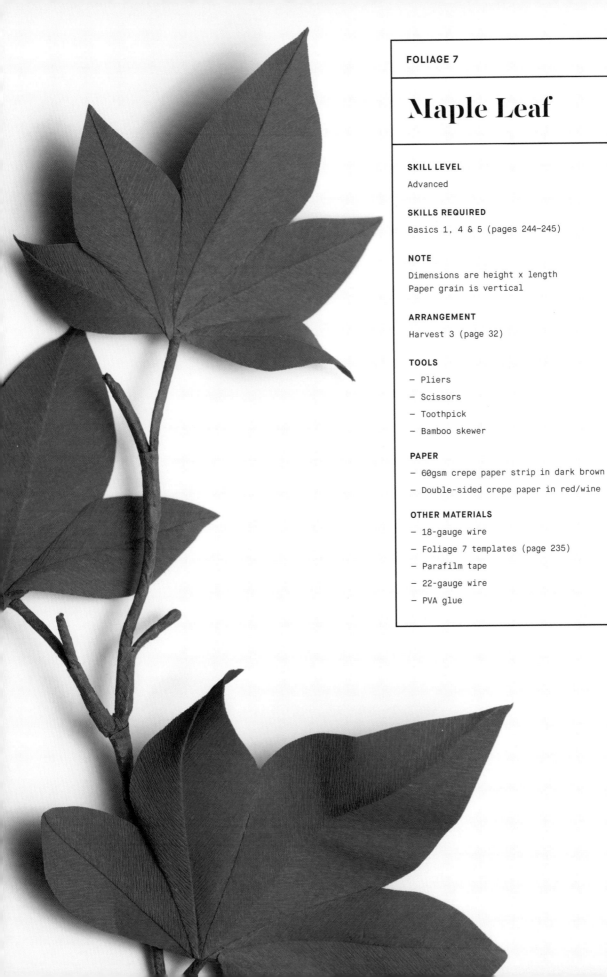

Maple Leaf

SKILL LEVEL
Advanced

SKILLS REQUIRED
Basics 1, 4 & 5 (pages 244–245)

NOTE
Dimensions are height x length
Paper grain is vertical

ARRANGEMENT
Harvest 3 (page 32)

TOOLS
- Pliers
- Scissors
- Toothpick
- Bamboo skewer

PAPER
- 60gsm crepe paper strip in dark brown
- Double-sided crepe paper in red/wine

OTHER MATERIALS
- 18-gauge wire
- Foliage 7 templates (page 235)
- Parafilm tape
- 22-gauge wire
- PVA glue

3

5

6

10

Stems

1. Cut three pieces of 18-gauge wire, each 40 cm (16 in) long. Bunch them together and wrap the entire length of the stem with parafilm tape. Cut nine pieces of 22-gauge wire, each 10 cm (4 in) long, then wrap each stem with parafilm tape. Wrap each of the 12 stems with dark-brown paper strip, securing with PVA glue.

Leaves

2. Using the red/wine double-sided paper and following the Basic Leaf method (page 219, steps 2–8), make the following: two leaves with template A; five leaves with template B; six leaves with template C; and two leaves with template D. In step 2 of the Basic Leaf method, change the dimensions of the double-sided paper to 18 x 9 cm (7 x 3½ in). Make sure the red side is facing up when folding. Separate the leaves by template.

LEAVES 1 & 2

3. You will need one A leaf, two B leaves, two C leaves and three of the short stems. Take one C leaf and, with the red side facing up, dab a small amount of PVA glue onto the lower right edge.

4. Take one B leaf and, with the red side facing up, place the lower left edge over the lower right edge of the C leaf. Gently press down to secure the join.

5. Continue to join leaves, in the following order: A-B-C. Flip the completed leaf over.

6. Using PVA glue, adhere three short stems to the leaf spines. Bunch the exposed wires together and wrap the entire length of the stem with dark-brown paper strip.

7. Repeat steps 3–6 to make a second leaf.

LEAF 3

8. Repeat steps 3–6 using one B leaf, two C leaves and two D leaves. Join the leaves in the following order: D-C-B-C-D.

Assembly

9. Take the long stem and gently bend the top 1.5 cm (½ in) at a 45-degree angle.

10. Using PVA glue, join the stem of leaf 3 to the top end of the long stem. Then join leaf 1 and leaf 2 to opposite sides of the stem, leaving 7–8 cm (2¾–3¼ in) between the nodes. Cover all the joins with dark-brown paper strip.

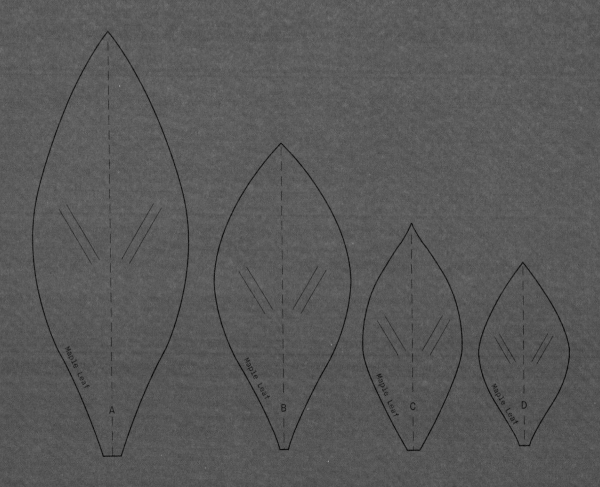

Maple Leaf

A

Maple Leaf

B

Maple Leaf

C

Maple Leaf

D

Olive Branch

SKILL LEVEL

Intermediate

SKILLS REQUIRED

Basics 1, 4 & 5 (pages 244–245)

NOTE

Dimensions are height x length
Paper grain is vertical

ARRANGEMENT

Frost 1 (page 40)

TOOLS

- Pliers
- Toothpick
- Scissors

PAPER

- 60gsm crepe paper strip in dark green
- 60gsm crepe paper in black
- Double-sided crepe paper in olive/
  moss green

OTHER MATERIALS

- 16-gauge wire
- 22-gauge wire
- PVA glue
- Foliage 8 templates (page 241)
- Cotton wool

2

3

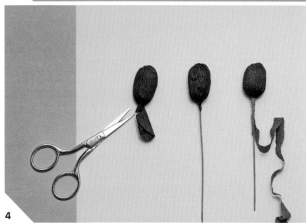

4

9

Stems

1. Cut one 25 cm (10 in) piece of 16-gauge wire. Then cut six pieces of 22-gauge wire, each 10 cm (4 in) long. Wrap the entire length of each stem with dark-green paper strip, securing with PVA glue.

Olives

2. Using black paper, cut one oval shape with template A. Gently cup, then place a small ball of cotton wool into the centre. Fold in the long sides and glue the edges together.

3. Twist both ends of the paper so that it resembles a wrapped sweet (candy). Press one end flat, then apply a small amount of glue between the top and bottom layers. Press firmly to secure. Apply glue to the top side of the flattened end, then fold it over to attach it to the olive.

4. Trim 1.5–2 cm (½–¾ in) from the other end, then untwist the paper. Using PVA glue, attach the olive to one end of a short stem. Cover the base of the olive with dark-green paper strip.

5. Repeat steps 2–4 to make two more olives.

Sprigs

6. Using olive/moss-green double-sided paper, cut nine leaves with template B.

7. Using PVA glue, attach the bottom 1 cm (½ in) of a leaf to one end of a short stem. Cover the base of the leaf with dark-green paper strip.

8. Attach a second leaf to the stem, 2 cm (¾ in) below the first leaf joint, and a third leaf 1 cm (½ in) below the second leaf joint. Cover the base of the leaves with dark-green paper strip.

9. Attach an olive to the sprig, 5 mm (¼ in) below the third leaf joint, leaving 2 cm (¾ in) between the base of the olive and the node. Cover the join with dark-green paper strip.

10. Repeat steps 6–9 to make two more sprigs.

Assembly

11. Using PVA glue, attach the bottom 3 cm (1¼ in) of a sprig to one end of the long stem. Attach a second sprig to the stem, 6 cm (2½ in) below the first sprig. Attach the third sprig to the stem, 6 cm (2½ in) below the node. Cover all the joins with dark-green paper strip.

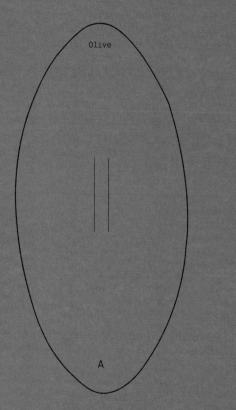

Olive

A

Olive

B

Skills

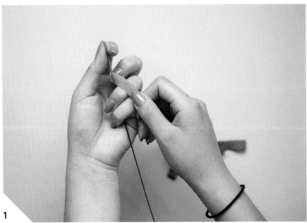

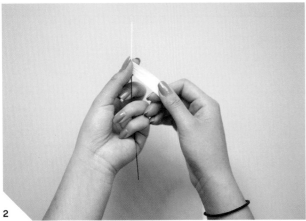

Basics

1. STEM WRAPPING WITH CREPE PAPER STRIP

In this book, we use two different weights of crepe paper to make strips: 180gsm and 60gsm. The 180gsm paper strip is used to thicken the flower stem, whereas the 60gsm paper strip is used to wrap the stem for finishing.

Note that these strips are not the same as the crepe paper 'streamers' you can buy from party suppliers, which are usually wider.

When cutting strips from a roll of crepe paper, make sure you cut across the grain and maintain a consistent width. Keep the length of your working strip to a 30 cm (12 in) maximum, especially if you are new to flower making.

To wrap a stem, first apply a small amount of PVA glue to one end of the stem, then attach one end of the paper strip. Hold the top of the stem with your thumb and index finger, while pressing the length of the stem against your palm with your pinkie and ring fingers. Wrap the paper strip around the stem in a downwards spiral, stretching the paper gently in the process. Wrap until the stem is completely covered, then cut away the excess paper. Secure the end of the strip with PVA glue.

2. STEM WRAPPING WITH TAPE

I prefer to use parafilm tape rather than florist tape, as parafilm tape is non-sticky and a lot easier to work with. Unless otherwise specified, the projects in this book use green parafilm tape.

Both florist tape and parafilm tape adhere by stretching, so stretch gently as you go. If this is your first time working with these tapes, it is best to cut them into short working strips of 20–25 cm (8–10 in).

To wrap a stem, first cover the top of the stem with tape. Hold the top of the stem with your thumb and index finger, while pressing the length of the stem against your palm with your pinkie and ring fingers. Wrap the tape around the stem in a downwards spiral, stretching the tape gently in the process. Wrap until the stem is completely covered, then tear off the excess tape. To secure the end of the tape, gently apply pressure around the bottom of the stem.

This technique is the most essential and challenging skill in flower making, so allow yourself plenty of time to practise. Once you have mastered this method, flower making will be a breeze.

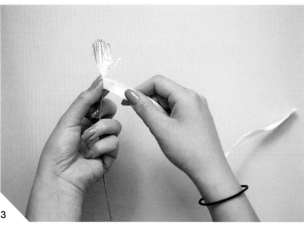

3

4

3. ATTACHING PETALS/LEAVES WITH TAPE

Use your thumb and index finger to secure the petal or leaf between the wire stem and the parafilm tape. Gently stretch the tape with your other hand, while wrapping the tape around the stem once. Tear off the excess tape, then apply pressure to secure the tape to the stem. Continue attaching the petals/leaves, tearing off the tape after each layer. If you are new to flower making, I recommend attaching one petal at a time. Once you are familiar with this technique, you can try securing multiple petals with one piece of tape.

4. ATTACHING PETALS/LEAVES WITH PVA GLUE

Using a toothpick, dab a small amount of PVA glue onto the bottom 5–10 mm (¼–½ in) of the petal or leaf. Place the base of the petal/leaf against the stem and gently apply pressure to secure. (To get the dried glue off your fingers without having to constantly wash your hands, apply hand lotion, then wipe it off using a dry towel.)

5. CUTTING SHAPES WITH TEMPLATES

The templates in this book are actual size, and the two lines on each template show the direction of the paper grain.

If you are new to flower making, I suggest cutting out one shape at a time using your templates. Once you have gained more control, you can cut multiple shapes at once by folding or stacking several pieces of paper together. When doing this, use a bulldog clip to secure the template to the layers of paper while cutting, moving the clip as you go.

6. PAPER PASTING

This technique is used when crepe paper needs to be thickened before use. Using a glue stick, cover the entire surface of one sheet with glue; use a minimal amount of glue to avoid discolouration. Place the second sheet on top of the first, making sure that the paper grain and edges are perfectly aligned. Use your palm to press the paper flat, smoothing the surface and securing the sheets together. Allow the paper to dry completely before cutting (this may take up to 30 minutes).

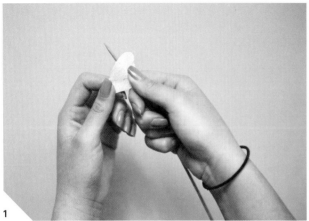

1

2

3

5

Shaping

1. CURLING

In this book, we curl using a bamboo skewer. However, curling can also be done using a pen or the end of a paintbrush. To curl a petal, hold the bottom of the petal with your thumb and index finger. Hold the bamboo skewer in your other hand. Place the middle of the petal between the skewer and your thumb, then gently draw the skewer outwards, curling the petal in the process.

2. CUPPING

Grasp the centre of the petal with both of your thumbs and index fingers. Press your thumbs against the paper while gently stretching outwards, so that the petal forms a concave shape. If you are new to flower making, I suggest cupping one petal at a time. Once you have mastered this skill, you can cup multiple petals at once by stacking several petals together.

3. FRINGING

Fringing can be done using fringing scissors or normal scissors. I recommend using normal scissors, as you will have more control over the shape and size of the fringe. Always cut along the grain when fringing.

4. RUFFLING

Hold the top edge of the petal between both of your thumbs and index fingers. Gently stretch the paper crosswise in small increments.

5. EDGE CUT-OUTS

Cut out a small inverted triangle anywhere on the top edge of the petal. Trim the pointy edges to make them round. Use the curling technique (above) to curl the scalloped edges. The trick to this technique is to embrace imperfection, as this will make your petals look more natural.

1A

1B

Colouring

1. FOOD DYE

In this book, we work with food dyes when dyeing paper, as they are safe, and absorb and dry quickly. (Alternatively, you could use coloured ink.) Dilute the food dye in water to the desired intensity. Always test the diluted dye on scrap paper, to make sure you have the right colour (note that some colours get darker once they dry). Below are two ways of colouring paper with dye.

A. Dry wash
Use a fan paintbrush to apply diluted dye directly onto a dry piece of crepe paper. Always paint along the grain. Allow the paper to dry completely before cutting it (this may take up to 30 minutes).

B. Wet wash
This technique is best used after you have cut the petals. Holding the bottom of a petal between your fingers, quickly dip the top 5 mm (¼ in) of the petal into plain water. Dip a paintbrush into the food dye, then lightly dab the brush along the top edge of the wet petal. You will see the colour start dripping down the petal. Allow the petal to dry completely before shaping (this may take up to 30 minutes).

2. EDGE DRAWING WITH A MARKER

Run the side of a marker along the very edge of a petal to create a coloured outline. If you are new to flower making, I suggest working with one petal at a time. Once you have mastered this skill, you can work with multiple petals at a time by stacking several petals together.

3. BLEACHING

When using bleach, always work in a well-ventilated area and wear protective equipment if necessary. First, dilute the bleach in water to the desired concentration — I usually use one part bleach to seven parts water. Dip a section of the paper in the diluted bleach. Allow the paper to dry completely before cutting (this may take several hours). Be aware that different products have different concentrations, so always test on scrap paper first to achieve the desired colour.

Tools & materials

1. Pliers

2. Edgers

3. Precision scissors

4. Scissors

5. Bamboo skewer

6. 16-gauge, 18-gauge and 22-gauge florist wire

7. Toothpicks

8. Ruler

9. Parafilm tape

10. Fan paintbrush

11. Round paintbrush

12. Flat paintbrush

13. 180gsm and 60gsm crepe paper:
    sold in rolls of 50 x 250 cm (20 x 100 in)

14. Ground turmeric

15. Artificial stamens

16. Cotton wool

17. Ground coffee

18. Glue stick

19. Coloured markers

20. Food dye

21. PVA glue

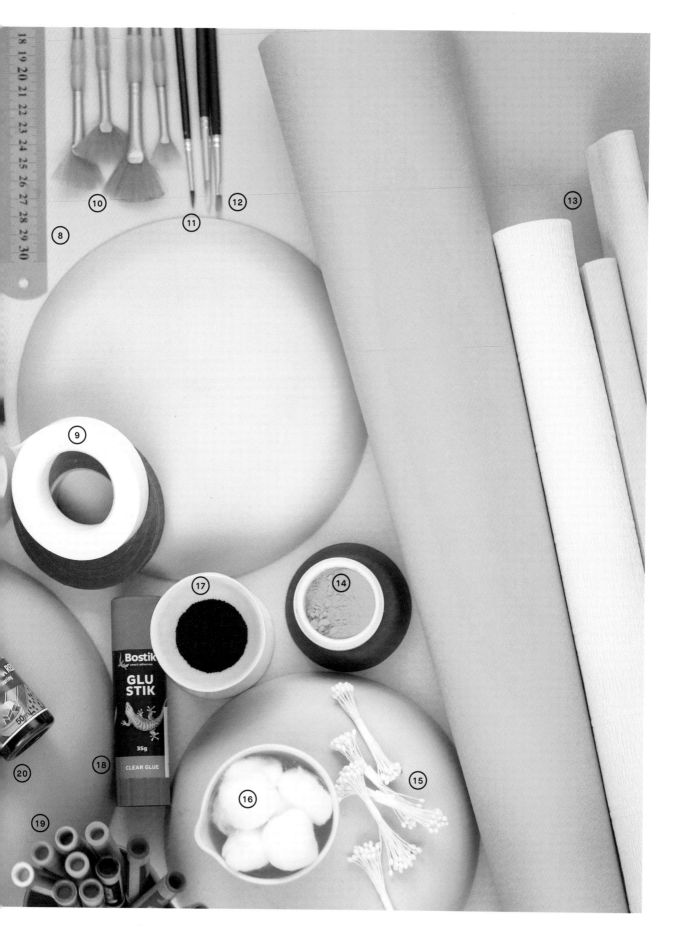

Suppliers

You can buy all the tools and materials you'll need (see page 248) from the following suppliers.

ART & CRAFT SUPPLIES

Australia: Etsy, Spotlight, Eckersley's Art & Craft
USA: Castle in the Air, Michaels
UK: Hobbycraft

FLORIST SUPPLIES

Australia: Etsy, Apack, Koch & Co, Spotlight
USA: Castle in the Air
UK: Michael Dark

PAPER

Australia: Etsy, l'uccello, RubyJu
USA: Carte Fini, Castle in the Air, Paper Mart
UK: Cartotecnica Rossi

TABLEWARE

Australia, USA & UK: Mud Australia (used throughout)

Acknowledgements

First and foremost, I would like to thank Kim Hungerford of Books Kinokuniya, Sydney, for realising my potential. Without her, this book would not exist.

My greatest appreciation goes to:

My mentor, Richard Aloisio, whose endless support has been paramount to my success. He is an incredible role model: a designer, a writer, a style inspiration and, above all, a wonderful friend. I am blessed to have him with me on this journey.

My mother, Le Hang, and the Nguyen-Tran family, for their care and sacrifices. Their legacy and strong belief in education have gotten me this far.

My assistant and hand model, My Linh Duong, for her unparalleled dedication and professionalism. Her contribution was crucial to the development of this book.

My production team for making it happen: Loran McDougall and Jane Willson of Hardie Grant Publishing. It was my honour and privilege to work with them.

I would also like to extend my gratitude to:

The Design Files, Design*Sponge and Etsy Australia, for launching my career.

Associate Professor Mark Raftery and Dr Carl Power of the University of New South Wales (UNSW), Australia, for their understanding and professional guidance.

Dr Kim Snepvangers and Associate Professor Bonita Ely for their attention and enormous support during my study at UNSW Art & Design.

My photography teacher, Michael Waite of the Australian Centre for Photography, for his invaluable lessons, encouragement and continuing support.

Photographer Dan Cheung of Angus Porter Photography, ceramicist Kei Takahashi and Shelley Simpson of Mud Australia for their generous loans of equipment and props.

To the most incredible and committed cheer squad, I love you all:

Sydney Liu Lau, Anastasia Korlimbinis, Trish McKay, Wei Ting Lee, Deisy Larios, Lynn Dolan, Tiffanie Turner, Kelsey Elam, Kate Alarcón, Anna Chedid, Tam Anh Le and Jisha Pareth Chali.

To Erik Backdahl, a special mention:

How could I start and end this book without you? Thank you for always believing in me and leading me in the right direction. Thank you for encouraging me to strive for excellence and to be the best I can be. Thank you for being there for me when I needed you. You are my best friend and a wonderful soul. This book is a celebration of our friendship — I promise to sign it on your 60th birthday.

About the author

Jennifer Tran is a flowersmith, an educator and the founder of Papetal. Since graduating from the University of New South Wales, Australia, with a Bachelor of Art Education and a Bachelor of Fine Arts (Hons), Jennifer's work has been featured in the *National Sculpture Magazine of China*, *Maker's Magazine* (Canada) and The Design Files (Australia). In early 2016, she was recommended by Design*Sponge as one of the top paper flower artists to follow. Jennifer's workshops at the Museum of Contemporary Art Australia and Books Kinokuniya in Sydney have been exceptionally well received. She is a frequent contributor to Etsy Australia and her online tutorials appear across multiple platforms. Jennifer's passion for the handmade is the foundation of this book.

Published in 2017 by Hardie Grant Books, an imprint of
Hardie Grant Publishing

Hardie Grant Books (Melbourne)
Building 1, 658 Church Street
Richmond, Victoria 3121

Hardie Grant Books (London)
5th & 6th Floors
52-54 Southwark Street
London SE1 1UN

hardiegrantbooks.com

A Cataloguing-in-Publication entry is available from
the catalogue of the National Library of Australia at
www.nla.gov.au

Flowersmith
ISBN 978 1 74379 291 9

Publishing Director: Jane Willson
Managing Editor: Marg Bowman
Project Editor: Loran McDougall
Editor: Jessica Redman
Design Manager: Mark Campbell
Designer: Murray Batten
Production Manager: Todd Rechner
Production Coordinator: Rebecca Bryson

Colour reproduction by Splitting Image Colour Studio
Printed in China by 1010 Printing International Limited